# Mama Moon

# Mama Moon
## A Testament To The Human Spirit

Susan Gayle

2009

# Mama Moon

CHAPTER I

Saturday, January 15, 2000. No different from any other day. The date didn't mark any special occasion. Yet I felt uneasy. A visionary flash? Hell no. I wish that were true. Perhaps the forewarning would have prepared me for things to come.

***

We are halfway to Atlantic City, the town that never sleeps, to get away for the weekend. Just as we cross the Delaware Memorial Bridge, I nonchalantly comment to my husband, Victor, who is driving, "I think I'll check our home voice mail." Not giving my comment a second thought, he nods in agreement, never breaking his concentration as he scans the traffic.

For a fleeting second I think, *What am I doing checking voice mail at two a.m.?* But there's nothing else to do but sit and watch cars and trucks pass by us for the next hour and half.

I dial our home voice mail number. "You have five new messages," the mechanical voice tells me.

I turn to Victor. "This is strange. Why would we have five new messages?" We didn't have any messages when we left home, and it was late then.

Victor looks at me curiously, his face guarded. He's had his share of bad news by phone.

I hold the phone close to my ear, bracing myself for the worst.

The messages are from my brother, Eddie. Except for the occasional hello, we haven't spoken for years. People may think that a bit odd considering we live so close to one another. I can hit his home with a stone from my driveway if I throw very hard. He's our father's namesake, Edward Donald. When he was younger, we called him Junior. Later, he adopted the nickname Eddie.

His voice sounds hollow and pleading: "Sue, call me."

*Now what does he want?* I wonder. It's never a good thing to hear from Eddie. My brother and I have little in common. He has real basic needs: eat, sleep, and crack cocaine.

And it isn't that he lacks the intelligence to do more with his life. His IQ tests place him in the genius category, from what I recall my mother telling me. Eddie, like so many other young males who are casualties of absentee fathers, turned to drugs to fill the void. At least that's what my mother and I believe.

Despite being a drug addict, Eddie always appears happy-go-lucky. And perhaps he is happy—until the crack cocaine, heroin, and God knows what else he's smoking, snorting, and shooting into his body wears off and he has to face his demons. His goal is to keep his addiction fed, day and night. Month after month. Year after year. Amazingly, after twenty years of drug abuse, he still looks healthy. He can talk intelligently, his eyes are clear, his teeth are strong and his gums are in good shape, and he has a lean, muscular physique.

Eddie's drug addiction has landed him in juvenile detention, jail, and prison. It has affected each member of our family, and we all handle it quite differently. I retreat from it. My sister accepts it. My mother fights it.

My mother's greatest love is Eddie. Her greatest heartbreak is Eddie. Motherhood is serious business to my mother; she doesn't take her job lightly. Her job was to raise her children to be self-sufficient and honest, to earn a decent living, and to live life to the fullest.

But when Eddie entered adulthood, my mother wasn't relieved of her "motherly duties." She wouldn't give up on him, as I have. My brother and mother are stuck in a time warp, with Eddie as the troubled teen and my mother as the pained but hopeful parent.

She's always bailing him out. No matter how much he steals from her. No matter how much he lies to her. No matter how much he breaks her heart. She never stops believing that "my Eddie"—as she calls him—will eventually straighten up, earn a college degree, own and operate a business, marry, and have children. Preferably in that order. Now *that* is asking for miracles.

My brother answers the phone immediately.

"You left several messages," I say. "Did something happen?"

"Mom was in a fire in Washington, DC," Eddie responds.

I go numb. In a steady voice, I ask, "Is she hurt?"

"There was an explosion," my brother stammers. He sounds like he's on something. Big surprise. "Mom and Artulo are at the Washington Hospital Burn Unit. Please, go to the hospital fast. I can't handle it no more."

He hangs up.

Artulo is my mother's husband. They married a little over a year ago.

Victor looks at me, waiting patiently.

"Eddie said that Mom was in a fire. I'm sure everything will be okay," I reply in a monotone voice.

Victor asks questions. I don't respond. My defenses are kicking in; protective walls spring up around me.

Each second feels like hours.

Sensing my anxiety, Victor says, "I'll turn the car around as soon as I can." Again, I don't respond. I know he wants to talk, but he knows me well enough to allow me time to think. He drives in silence.

I begin mentally preparing myself for the worst. My mother already has medical problems. Her lymph nodes do not function properly due to the radiation used to treat the cancer she had years ago. Her right leg will double in size just from standing too long. God forbid if she cuts her foot and it becomes infected. What will severe burns do to her leg?

I wonder what her life will be like in a wheelchair. She's so damned independent. I just can't envision her helpless. *What about me? Me, the caretaker?* I see myself pushing her, depressed and slumped over, in a wheelchair. Then, guiltily, I question why I'm thinking of myself.

I nestle within the protective walls that allow me to think about this unbelievable situation in a coherent way. Thoughts begin swirling in my head.

I'm not able to reach any conclusions. There are many unknowns. So thoughts continue to bounce and roll around in my head.

Around, around, around.

*Make sense of this.*

*Make sense of this.*

***

If we are lucky, we'll be able to make it to the hospital in two hours. I grow increasingly anxious being so close, yet so far. I want to hold Mom's hand and comfort her. She is probably terrified, wondering where I am.

Although it seems like hours, I hung up with Eddie only a few minutes ago. I call the hospital where I'm transferred from one department to the next until I finally reach the doctor treating my mother and Artulo.

"Your mother and father are seriously injured," he tells me. "They were burned in a building in Washington, DC. We believe they were in-

3

jured in some type of explosion. I'll provide you with more details when I see you in person at the hospital."

"Will she survive?" I ask, keeping my emotions in check. But my chest feels like a dam about to burst.

"We'll talk when you arrive," repeats the doctor.

"Okay, thank you," I say matter-of-factly. "We should be there in a couple of hours."

How can I remain so calm? I feel like screaming, *Just tell me, will she live or not?* A simple yes or no would suffice. It takes everything in me not to behave like an insane person.

If my mother truly had been seriously injured, surely my sixth sense would have alerted me. I wouldn't have gone to work. I wouldn't have eaten. I wouldn't have smiled, or laughed. So her injuries can't be really, really bad. Bad, perhaps, but not fatal.

I try to be optimistic while I can. What good will it do to be otherwise? I have a choice, and I choose optimism. I won't have a choice when I come face-to-face with the facts of my mother's condition. It will have to be what it is. I hope and pray that the reality will turn out to be good news.

Thoughts continue to race and run together in my head, streams of melted wax randomly zigzagging down a candlestick.

*My mother will be okay. She's such a strong woman. She would never die like this. It's going to be tough for her if she is confined to a wheelchair. But she'll make do. Just like she always has.*

*Yes, she'll make it. My mother is a fighter. She's been through far worse. Nothing gets her down. Nothing.*

***

My thoughts turn to the past. My past. My mother's past.

I'm going back. Far back—where it's safe and predictable.

I'm still breathing, yet I feel as though I'm experiencing what has been described as a "near-death experience." I am present, but hovering somewhere in the corner of the room, like an insect trapped in a spider's web. Random, nonsensical thoughts play through my mind, silly philosophical ramblings: *how does one nearly die?*

I don't want to feel anything until I know for sure my mother is all right. I want to keep negative thoughts away from me, shoo them away like pesky flies.

*Just stay focused. Stay in control,* I think, to comfort myself. *Don't let this overwhelm you.*

My childhood begins playing in slow motion. I remember. Since the day I was old enough to comprehend language, my mother would tell me about her past, her life before I was born. When her past caught up to my birth, she would tell me events that I couldn't remember. Even when I was a youngster, I knew my mother's life was different from most people's lives.

Back. Back. Far back.

My head is resting on the car's headrest. I stare straight ahead with unseeing eyes.

Now I'm in survival mode, the drums in my head beating *nothing bad, nothing bad.*

I reassure myself, *We can get through this, whatever it is.*

Cars, tractor-trailers, streetlights, guard railings, and trees alongside Interstate 95 fade into the night.

CHAPTER 2

My mother's stories are strewn about my memory like pieces of a puzzle. I need to start piecing the puzzle together to create coherency out of the chaos that is swirling around in my head. What picture will emerge? At this very moment, I'm not sure of much of anything.

My mother still has a heavy Korean accent, despite living in the U.S. for decades. Nevertheless, I have always understood her. She attended English language classes but found herself falling asleep in class or not being able to understand the instructors. Her language handicap had been a lifelong struggle. She was ashamed that she couldn't learn to speak English clearly.

For as long as I can remember, I have given my mother advice about all sorts of matters, personal and business. I don't ever recall her talking to me as if I were a child. Of course, my highly opinionated mother didn't always agree with me. She thought I worried too much, that I didn't take enough risks, that I was too conservative. That I needed to expose myself more to life in order to *really live life* to the fullest.

I would always respond, "Well, that's why I don't have the problems you have. I like to live a peaceful, calm life. You need to slow down and quit driving yourself and everyone around you crazy." I wanted something different for my mother. I just wanted her to be happy and at peace with herself. She always seemed to take on more than she could handle, and I was powerless to stop her.

My mother would just laugh. "Sujan, you are so smart, but not so smart about business. You have to take risks if you really want to live life. There is plenty of time to rest when you die." She didn't shield me from the harshness of reality. She wanted me to be strong. To believe in myself. To make the world a better place.

"You can do whatever you want. Don't 'talkee' about it, just do it," she would say. She didn't believe in waste. So why waste her life lessons by keeping them to herself?

Our mother-daughter talks were, at times, soul wrenching. Other times, we were like two girlfriends giggling and sharing secrets. My mother wasn't one to hide much. What you saw was what you got. She had experienced many hardships in her lifetime, but remained optimistic and appreciative of things many people take for granted. She loved to share her life lessons and philosophies with me, and she wanted me to learn how to appreciate and not waste opportunities to improve myself, to help others in need, and to improve the world in which we all lived, for future generations.

These mother-daughter talks created the lenses from which I viewed my world. I knew I would never experience the hardships she had experienced. But I did learn how to be grateful and thankful for what I had learned from my mother's experiences. She was born into a place and in an era, which in themselves would test her endurance.

Hardship is relative. My life was easy compared to my mother's life, and she would constantly remind me of how lucky I was.

Lucky to be living in "this wonderful country," the United States.

Lucky to be able to receive an education.

Lucky to be able to read and write.

Lucky to have two arms and two legs.

Lucky to be able to eat anything I wanted, whenever I wanted.

Lucky to be able to work hard and become whatever I chose to be.

Throughout the years, my mother would tell me bits and pieces about her life. It was as if she felt that exposing too much of her life story at one time would be too much for her to handle, and too much for me to comprehend.

CHAPTER 3

My mother was born on July 15, 1932, in Taejon, Korea. Named Moon Ja, she was the third daughter out of seven surviving siblings—six sisters and one brother—in her family, the Yang family. Mom's father's name was Bok and her mother's name was Kil Sung.

The Yang family had typical Korean physical features—the square, well-defined jaw line, nicely shaped noses, and flawless skin. The women had almond-shaped eyes.

The Yang family was very close-knit, and the six Yang sisters and Kil Sung coddled the one and only boy. As in most Asian counties, in Korea the male child is an exalted position, mainly because he can carry the family name to the next generation. At the same time, however, the Yang sisters didn't hesitate to give brother Yang a harsh tongue-lashing if he didn't live up to the Yang name.

My grandfather Bok was tall by Korean standards. He reportedly stood over six feet tall. My grandmother Kil Sung was a tiny figure of a woman, standing only four feet five inches.

My mother's family was poor, not out of laziness by any means. Bok held a couple of low-paying positions during his lifetime. He received a commission for brokering the sale of pigs and other livestock. Later, he dug ditches for installing main water pipes—a dangerous job. The dirt walls caved in, quickly burying Bok.

Luckily, his height saved him. His head remained above the dirt that trapped his body, so he could breathe, albeit with difficulty because his body was being pressed on all sides by the dirt. Mother said he had respiratory problems from that day forward.

Kil Sung had little time to rest. She fed and clothed her seven children while pregnant through most of her childbearing years. She had many, many miscarriages; at one time, a relative reported ten! It was a way of life for Korean women in that era. She worked day and night just to clothe and feed her family, sewing her children's clothes by hand. My mother told me that when the clothes needed washing, my grandmother would take apart their clothing seam by seam, wash each piece of material by hand, and then sew the materials back together, again and again and again.

In 1943, when the Japanese government had a strong presence in Tae-jon City, the Japanese employed my mother at the tender age of eleven. My Uncle Yang told me, decades later, that my mother performed office work for the Japanese government. From what I understood about her duties, she was an office "gopher." *Go deliver this. Go clean this. Go fetch us this.* She gave her meager earnings to her father to feed the family. He said that it made the difference between the Yang family starving and surviving.

A year later, Mom landed another job. She mixed solutions to make eye medicine as the assistant to a Japanese ophthalmologist, and grew very close to the ophthalmologist and his wife.

In 1945, the Japanese evacuated Korea. The Japanese were the Korean people's worst enemy, and so Korea became a very hostile place for Japanese to live. The ophthalmologist's family fled Korea with no time to spare, but before fleeing, they posted a public notice on their residence's front door assigning ownership of their property to my mother. She was very pleased to receive such a valuable gift, and couldn't wait to share her good fortune with her family. Naturally, she would turn the property over to her father.

But Bok's reaction was unexpected. He was outraged that my mother would even think of accepting a gift from a Japanese person. He ranted and raved about all things Japanese being evil. Yet my mother had a difficult time believing him. She had a wonderful experience with her former Japanese employers and was grateful they'd hired her, allowing her to financially support her family.

My mother was also frustrated that she didn't have a "voice." Outwardly, she obeyed her father's command, but inwardly, she didn't agree with her father's decision. She also struggled with the way he sacrificed his family's needs in order to preserve his pride. My mother was able to discard tradition and custom when faced with death from a shortage of the most basic need—food. Nothing else mattered.

Another death threat was a very real possibility of the Japanese "enlisting" my mother to serve the Japanese soldiers in their field camps. Stories abounded about Japanese soldiers stealing Koreans, including pretty, young, and single women, who were called "comfort girls." These young captives cooked, cleaned, and satisfied the sexual needs of Japanese soldiers. They traveled with the soldiers from camp to camp. History has captured horror stories of the treatment of these "comfort girls," including vicious gang rapes, severe beatings, and torture, all too often resulting in their premature death. "Comfort girls" became the property of their captives, discarded like pieces of trash when they were no longer wanted.

My mother, while spared of that horror, encountered several Japanese soldiers who stopped their vehicle when they spotted her walking alongside a road and raped her. She was thankful they spared her life. She mentioned this only once, and I didn't probe because I could sense the event was a closed topic from that day forward. I'm not even certain how old she was, or if she reported the incident. I imagine that telling anyone would have brought only shame on herself and her family.

My grandfather wanted to ensure that my mother didn't meet the fate of a "comfort girl," so he arranged for her to be married as soon as possible. It wasn't long before he found a suitable Korean husband to marry her.

\*\*\*

My grandparents married my mother to Tae Hyun Yeo, a local businessman, who would provide security for her well-being and protect her from the evil Japanese soldiers. Mr. Yeo was twenty-three years old and my mother was sixteen when they married. He was a good catch, as he had the financial means to provide my mother with a home, food, and security. I've heard that he owned a couple of businesses, a bicycle repair shop, and later a shoe store.

Using surnames may sound formal, but it was the polite way to refer to people in the Korean culture. Koreans also would refer to their family members as mother (*oma*), father (*haba-chee*), husband or sweetheart (*yobo*), and siblings by birth order: sister (*onee*) number one, sister number two, and so on.

What did love have to do with it? Nothing, when it came to marriages arranged by well-intended parents. Mr. Yeo could financially care for my mother and keep her safe from the Japanese. Times were hard. If Mr. Yeo could just provide the basics for survival, that's all that mattered. My mother didn't love Mr. Yeo, but that wasn't important. She only needed to honor her parents' decision to maintain her standing as a good daughter.

Soon after the marriage ceremony, however, my mother saw a much darker side to her husband. He was mean-spirited, controlling, and violent. Mom hadn't expected to fall in love, but she also hadn't expected to be beaten daily. She had mistakenly believed that Mr. Yeo was her savior. Instead, she had been placed into the hands of an enemy. Again, she found that she didn't have a voice. Men ruled in Korea, in all aspects of life.

Women considered themselves fortunate if they were married to a man who treated them with kindness.

Due to her upbringing, my mother was submissive to Mr. Yeo. By sheer willpower, however, she quietly remained independent in her thoughts and opinions. There was no need for Mr. Yeo to beat a willing participant into submission. Yet he found the most trivial of excuses to dominate her, be it through his fists, words, or control of what and how much she ate. My mother blamed Mr. Yeo's opium addiction for his violent outbursts.

She told me about a time that particularly stuck out in her memory. Mr. Yeo noticed a small hole in the rice paper wall and accused my mother of looking outside without his permission. He yanked her to the floor by her hair, held her there, and hit her with his fist, shouting, "You are a bad wife!" Without loosening his grip, he grabbed a tool like a screwdriver and wrapped her hair around it. He used the tool as a tourniquet, twisting her hair with it until she could feel the hair starting to rip from her scalp. She said it felt as if her scalp were on fire.

My mother told me this story several times when I was a youngster. Each time she relived those horrifying moments, she would ask no one in particular, "How can a human treat another human so mean? In the United States, people treat their dogs better than my Korean husband treated me."

What seemed to bother her more than the beatings, though, were her feelings of shame for conceding to Mr. Yeo in an attempt to calm him. She would apologize over and over again. She told me, "I was a stupid woman for saying, 'I'm sorry.' Why should I say I sorry? I listen to my husband. I clean the house. I cook. I have his baby. I no bad wife. I good wife."

I asked my mother how she was able to continue to try to be a good wife to Mr. Yeo after all that he had done to her. She explained that by being a good wife she was honoring her parents. If her husband wasn't pleased, then she was a bad daughter. My mother feared that she would bring shame on her parents. Staying with Mr. Yeo also meant she could hoard rice from their meager ration to give to her family.

Another story stands out. As did all good Korean wives, my mother walked several paces behind her husband, with her head bent slightly downward and her eyes partially lowered to the ground. She would greet neighbors with a bow when they passed by, accompanied by a polite greeting. She had to be very careful that she wasn't overly friendly when greeting male neighbors. Otherwise, she would have to pay the consequences of "flirting" with a man.

There were many instances where Mr. Yeo believed my mother's innocent greeting or glance toward a male to be inappropriate. As soon as they stepped into the privacy of their home, Mr. Yeo would direct a barrage of jealous accusations at her. She didn't know what to say, so she avoided making eye contact and remained silent, not wanting to appear to be disagreeable. It would only make matters worse.

She knew the pattern. First the accusations. Then the punches. She tried to be as submissive as possible in order not to fuel Mr. Yeo's rage. Her body tensed, readying her muscles and bones for the beating. Her mind stayed focused on one thought: *He can kill me, but he can't kill my spirit.*

\*\*\*

A year after my mother married, she gave birth to a son. His name was Woon Gee. He was thin and sickly and had upper respiratory problems. My mother thought it was probably due to poor nourishment. Breast milk would have helped his health, but my mother couldn't produce any, perhaps because she too was undernourished, or because she was under tremendous stress. Or both. We'll never know for sure, but both theories sound perfectly reasonable.

Mr. Yeo showed no more compassion for his first child than he had for his wife. As he had controlled my mother's food ration, so he did with his newborn son. When my mother talked to me about trying to find food for her firstborn child, she looked despondent. She said she would never forget their first winter together. By then, Woon Gee was eight months old. He cried from hunger pangs day and night. The cries would turn into whimpers, a constant reminder to my mother that she was inadequate. She couldn't even feed her son.

My mother told me that she had to prepare meals outdoors. She described one particular winter night as "so black I couldn't see my hand in front of me," and "so cold that my whole body shook and my fingers became numb with cold." Shaking and numbed by the cold, she attempted to light a fire, but couldn't keep it going. After several unsuccessful attempts, my mother just wanted to lie down on the ground and die. She couldn't please her husband. She couldn't feed her son. She guiltily thought, *What kind of wife and mother am I?* But then she said to herself, *I want to live. My son has to live.*

Squatting again on the cold ground with renewed determination, my mother finally lit the fire. She placed the pan of leftover rice over the fire, and as the water started boiling, she scraped hardened rice from the sides of the pan. The boiling rice turned into a milky, soupy mixture, which my mother carefully spoon-fed to Woon Gee. He ate the starchy mixture as if it was his last meal, but it would only satisfy his hunger for a short while. Poor, poor baby. She wished she could do more.

Shortly after giving birth, my mother had begun planning her escape, a daunting task. If Mr. Yeo found her, he would surely kill her. And where would she go? How would she get there in this war-torn county? What would she do once she was safe from Mr. Yeo? The unknown, although greatly feared, gave her a chance of survival. The mere thought of escaping made her heart shake, which would be her body's reaction to stress many, many years later. Doctors diagnosed the symptoms as panic attacks.

Many Korean women tolerated these conditions. During those times in Korea, there were no safety nets, like battered women's shelters or sympathetic laws. Women were considered the property of their husbands. So without the Yeo name, my mother didn't exist as a wife or a mother. Despite all of this, she chose the life of an outcast rather than stay in an abusive marriage.

She waited until Mr. Yeo left the house, and as soon as she could no longer see the back of his head, she hurriedly prepared for her escape. Perspiring and breathing hard, she packed food and a few articles of clothing, then secured Woon Gee to her back by wrapping a wide swath of cloth around him and tying it at around her chest and stomach. Then she left. Her feet and back ached from carrying Woon Gee and her belongings on her trek to freedom. Finally, she reached her destination, her parents' home, where they could live in peace.

However, peace was wishful thinking. When she arrived on her parents' doorstep and they learned why she and the baby were there, she was not welcomed with open arms. She had made her parents ashamed. She had brought shame on their entire family. My mother was no longer a Yang. Like livestock, she had been given to the Yeo family. Her father's honor was more important to him than my mother's life.

"Go to your husband's home!" her parents ordered. "You should be happy that you have food to eat. You must have been a bad girl for Mr. Yeo to treat you like that." They insisted that she return to where she belonged and be a good wife.

It didn't take long for Mr. Yeo to recover his property, my mother and his son. At least my mother felt she finally had done something that warranted a sound beating. Mr. Yeo placed her under house arrest, and she knew it was only a matter of time before he would kill her. Still, as much as he tried, he couldn't destroy her spirit. She never stopped dreaming of the day she would escape from this seemingly never-ending nightmare.

Eventually, Mr. Yeo allowed my mother to visit her family again. She relished those times when she could experience love and laugher, even for a fleeting moment. My mother always brought as much rice as she could spare and risk taking from her own household ration. It wasn't easy hiding things from Mr. Yeo. Out of her meager household ration, she would stash a small amount of rice in a tin can, in anticipation of her upcoming visits with her family. The large Yang family could always use more rice.

My mother always journeyed on foot to visit her family, with Woon Gee strapped to her back. She would select a route with the fewest number of people because she was ashamed for them to see her walking in shoes three sizes too big, especially in a country where small feet on a woman are attractive. She didn't want to look like a *coogee-girl*, a beggar. So whenever possible, instead of walking over bridges, she would walk around bridge embankments or through shallow water under bridges, all the while guarding her precious can of white rice.

\*\*\*

The day finally arrived when she felt brave enough to run away from Mr. Yeo again. His beatings were becoming increasingly more violent; this decision was a matter of survival—she had to leave. She wasn't ready to die. Her fear had turned to hate. Hate for the man who beat her. Hate for the man who left her no choice but to abandon her firstborn child. Hate for the man who took away her bright-eyed innocence. Decades later, my mother would practically spit when she said the name Yeo.

She knew that she would have to run fast and far this time. She realized she couldn't tell her family that she was fleeing. They would feel it was their duty to help Mr. Yeo find her. To make matters worse, she also knew she couldn't take her baby with her. How would she feed him? He would be safer remaining with Mr. Yeo than possibly face starving to death. Both my mother and her son's chances of survival were better if she left him with Mr. Yeo.

Mom's heart ached as she looked at her little boy, who was only one or maybe two years old, for what she knew might be the last time. Telling me about it, she still couldn't believe she had been capable of leaving her son. She'd asked herself over and over, "How can I leave my son?" She knew that once she left Mr. Yeo, Woon Gee would no longer be her child. He, like my mother, belonged to the Yeo family. Even the Korean officials didn't recognize my mother's claim to Woon Gee without Mr. Yeo's acknowledgement. She was simply the vessel for giving birth to a male child who would carry on the Yeo name.

Before departing, she whispered softly to her only child, "I love you, Woon Gee. I try to find you again. You grow up to be strong, smart boy. I love you." Tears streamed down her face, reflecting her broken heart. As anguished as she felt, something inside of her said, urgently and loudly, "Flee or you'll die."

So my mother ran away. She hid at various friends' homes in or around Pusan, Korea, moving regularly so Mr. Yeo couldn't find her. She would hear from friends that Mr. Yeo was searching for her, but eventually he simply gave up and moved on. He erased her from his life. She was no longer the mother of his son. In fact, she was never married to him, according to the official government family census records. Mr. Yeo remarried a few times after his first marriage to my mother.

I am not certain how many years later my mother met my father, Ed. In any case, she met him somewhere between the time Woon Gee reached a year old (1950) and I was born (1955). My father was four years older than my mother. Her girlfriend, who was dating an American soldier, introduced Mom to Ed.

Dad was also an enlisted soldier in the U.S. Army. Only "bad" girls dated American soldiers, but my mother had been through too much to simply accept tradition without question. If it made good sense or just felt right, she did it. Just as she thought it had been silly for her father not to accept a gift from a Japanese person, she didn't see why she couldn't date a man who treated her well just because he was American. She no longer cared about pleasing others. Yes, Mr. Yeo's beatings taught her something: survival is king!

Due to the language barrier, my mother and father's verbal communication was limited, but that didn't stop their relationship and love from growing. Ed knew enough Korean to be able to communicate. He was the complete opposite of Mr. Yeo. He treated my mother with respect and kindness, and they built their relationship on trust.

Ed and Moon in Korea

When my mother attempted to wash my father's feet, he kindly pushed her away. He tried to explain that she was not his maid but rather his partner. At first, she thought he was rejecting her attempts to show respect and affection. But she soon realized that he was falling in love with her for the person she was, not for the services she could provide.

Eventually, they moved in together in a small home in Pusan. She finally felt safe. He treated her with kindness, and she had shelter and plenty of food. She was extremely grateful to him for providing her with the basic essentials of life: food and shelter. He was also a generous man. Although his enlisted grade in the military pay scale was minimal, an American dollar was worth its weight in gold in Korea. My mother believed herself to be rich and a very lucky woman to have met Ed. She was overjoyed to have escaped Mr. Yeo's brutal beatings. And she was particularly happy that she would be able to help her family during a period when many Koreans starved to death.

Ed and Moon in Korea

My mother felt a deep sense of obligation to help her family, the Yangs, with food, clothing, and other sundry items that would make their lives more comfortable. She wanted to share her good fortune with them. Unannounced, she visited her parents' home for the first time since leaving Mr. Yeo, bringing them American food, clothing, and money.

Once again, instead of a joyful reunion, my mother was greeted with her father's outrage. "You bring shame to the Yang name. You live with American. You bring American money to our home—that mean you bring trouble to our home. You not my daughter!" he shouted. So from that day forward, my mother no longer belonged to the Yang family. Just as Mr. Yeo denounced her existence, my mother's father also disowned her. She no longer existed.

Mom didn't let her father's words deter her, although they hurt her deeply. She was determined to provide her family with the basic essentials they needed to survive. To avoid bringing shame to her father, she would schedule her visits late at night, when most neighbors were sleeping. When she arrived at the house, her father would leave the room. He stopped speaking to her because she no longer existed. But if she had stopped bringing food and money, as I learned years later from my Korean uncle, the family would have starved to death. My uncle said that they would ration their food between my mother's visits. If she arrived a day later than anticipated, they would be without food for that day.

When my mother told me about the hard time her father gave her, I grew angry. She, however, would have no part of my anger or disrespect for my then deceased Korean grandfather. Patiently, she explained that Koreans saw mixing races as killing the pure Korean race. Koreans have a long-term view and are always working toward making things better for future generations. That thinking extends to all aspects of their lives, be it improving family genetics or increasing their wealth for posterity. What's good for your children and grandchildren is what is good for parents (because they live through their children, who live through their children, and so on to infinity).

This explains why Korean mothers are not outwardly affectionate with their children. My mother said that when Korean mothers kiss their children, it is like kissing their own arm. If you want to be viewed as modest, an honorable trait in Korea, you don't make physical displays of affection to family members in public.

\*\*\*

I was born on March 7, 1955. My mother was twenty-two years old and my father was twenty-six. He encouraged my mother to give me a Korean name, although she disagreed, insisting that I should have an American name because I was American. They agreed to name me Susan.

Moon Ja holding Susan

At the time of my birth, my half-brother Woon Gee was five years old. He would be turning six in less than a week.

Soft curls framed my round face and large brown eyes. My hair was light brown. My mother loved dressing me up, sometimes in a traditional Korean dress.

My mother, and later my Korean aunts, told me that when they took me for walks in the villages, Koreans in the streets would stop in their tracks to look at me, exclaiming, *"Epoda!"* (pretty). On closer inspection, they realized that my race was mixed. Then they would ask, *"Mee Gook?"* (American?). But they didn't wait for a response. A few seconds later, they would say with confidence, *"Mee Gook."* While the meaning seemed harmless enough, their intonation indicated disapproval of my mother and father's union. Interestingly, American soldiers' racial epithet for Koreans was "Gook," which is actually the Korean word for "country."

My mother's sisters, however, accepted me regardless of my mixed-race status. From all accounts, they loved me. I do not recall having a relationship with my Korean grandparents, and I imagine that my grandfather viewed my birth with disdain, just another black mark on the Yang name.

My mother recognized that my life in Korea would not be easy. Korean society would treat me like a second-class citizen if we continued to live there. I would not be able to receive a good education. It was more important than ever that she take me to the United States. That is where I belonged, in my father's homeland.

CHAPTER 4

On February 5, 1958, nearly three years after my birth, my father married my mother. Shortly after their marriage, he received military orders to return to the United States. He promised that he would take care of the paperwork necessary to bring us to join him.

How could my mother know for sure that my father would keep his promise? She had witnessed the growing number of Korean women and their babies deserted by American soldiers, who returned to the U.S. without further communication. More often than not, the old saying was true: *out of sight, out of mind.*

My mother worried that Ed might have an American girlfriend waiting for him and that he would forget about us as soon as he landed on U.S. soil. Or perhaps his parents would be opposed to him marrying a Korean woman. If my father abandoned Mom and me in Korea, how would she care for us? She could always remarry, but a decent Korean man wouldn't want her because she had an American child. These thoughts, among others, caused her many a sleepless night.

On the other hand, no man had ever treated my mother as well as my father did. She trusted him. "Ed have good heart," she would say. "He honest and good man."

My father temporarily moved into his parents' home in Cambridge, New York. My mother and father wrote letters to one another frequently through a Korean interpreter. My father would refer to my mother as *yobo*, which meant "sweetheart" in Korean. He wrote love letters to my mother and reassured her that they'd be reunited very soon.

Mom sent my father a picture of me at almost three years old. I am standing with my small arms stiffly at my sides, dressed in a traditional Korean silk dress: long, colorful, flowing, and a short jacket with full sleeves striped in the primary colors. The picture shows off my soft curly hair and round face. My expression is one of surprise.

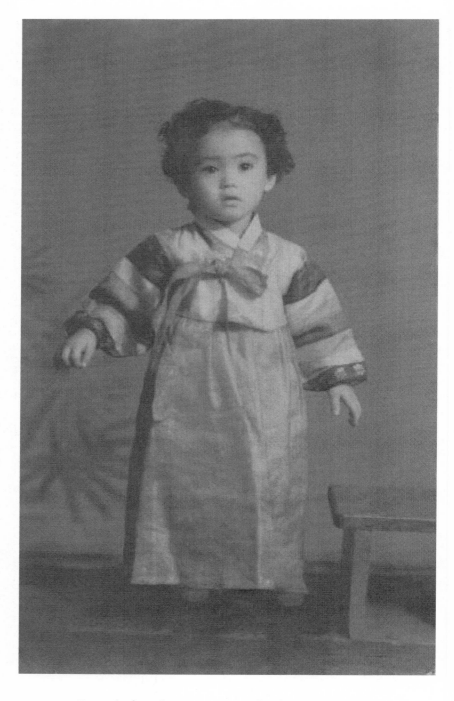

Susan before departing Korea for the United States

When my father received my picture in the mail, he proudly showed it to his family in New York. My American grandparents commented that I looked like a little Korean doll, and my mother must have seen that comment as the highest of compliments because she mentioned it to me throughout the years, always with a look of pride.

\*\*\*

My father kept his promise to my mother. On June 11, 1958, she and I left Korea to journey to an unfamiliar and strange land, a continent away, leaving behind the only family we knew. My mother had placed all of her trust in another person, something she had promised herself she would never do again. My father was her sole lifeline in a vast ocean of unknowns. She had no idea how to navigate in the U.S. She had no family. She had no friends. But her biggest obstacle was the language barrier. She could not speak or write in English.

Although going to the U.S. was a dream come true, my mother had mixed emotions. She would miss her family and friends. She would miss the familiarity of her life. She would miss her country.

But her logic, always dominant over her emotions, said that this move was a good thing. Good for her, and good for her American daughter. Good for her family's financial well-being as well. There was no point in crying. It was time to move on!

Always thinking of her family's best interests, my mother suggested to her father that it would be good for her brother to come with us to the U.S. She said that she and Ed could adopt him as their son so that he could become a U.S. citizen. She wanted her brother to receive a good education in one of the many universities in the States.

However, Bok refused to allow his only son to immigrate to the U.S. He feared that he would never see him again. My mother pleaded with her father to do what was best for her brother's future and allow him to leave with her, but Bok wouldn't change his mind. She had no choice but to leave her brother behind.

Nevertheless, she didn't give up. If she couldn't bring him to the States to get a good education, she would find a way to pay for his education in Korea. Her dreams for her brother's future continued. One day, not too far in the future, she hoped to be able to provide him with a good education.

I have pondered on how different my Korean uncle's life might have turned out if he left Korea with us, decades earlier. Would he be the owner of a small struggling business, as is his current situation? Or, would he be a college grad working on Wall Street?

I'm not certain how my American grandparents initially felt about my father marrying a Korean woman, but by the time we arrived, they welcomed us warmly. My paternal grandparents lived in Cambridge, New York, in a country setting. They had a cozy farm-style home with a big inviting porch, where they lived a comfortable middle-class existence.

My American grandfather's ancestry was French. He was short and somewhat stocky, with thinning hair and a ruddy nose and cheeks. He seemed quiet and gentle. He had married a full-blooded Irishwoman, also short, and with a kind, round face. Always smiling, she was energetic, outgoing, and warm. Both of my American grandparents showered me with love and attention.

I loved to sit on my grandfather's lap and comb his thinning hair. My grandmother was always cooking in the kitchen. In the early morning, I would wake to the smell of eggs and bacon frying in an old-fashioned iron skillet. After breakfast, I would play in a homemade sandbox for most of the day, making mud pies.

Susan brushing her American Grandfather's hair

When my father received his next military orders, we moved to Fort Dix in New Jersey. My brother, Edward Jr., was born a year later, on June 29, 1959. He was a chubby-cheeked baby; my mother used to tell us that he was so fat he couldn't roll over on his own.

My father worked long hours to keep us financially afloat, and Mom was grateful to him for giving us a secure, comfortable life. She wanted to be a good wife. She wanted to be a good mother. She had achieved her dreams, except for one: ensuring that her children and her brother received good college educations. Other than that, she was satisfied to be Edward Catellier's wife and the mother of her children through eternity. She couldn't have asked for a better life.

My father pampered her. He certainly didn't fit the domineering Korean male stereotype that she had grown up accepting. He thought it only fair that he share in the domestic duties—unheard of in Korea—where cleaning the home, cooking, and caring for children were clearly the wife's duties. My father also encouraged Mom to go to English classes. As motivated as she was to learn to speak and write English, she just couldn't quite grasp the language.

Because she could barely speak English, she made few friends among the mostly Caucasian military wives, and it didn't help that she was shy. Her social contacts were limited to her immediate family. The few friendships that she did have were short-lived, since we moved frequently. Such was the life of a military family.

Mom kept herself busy by cooking, cleaning, and sewing for the better part of the day. Sewing was her passion, and it provided her with a creative outlet. She sewed our clothes, curtains, bedspreads, among other articles. She also was very skilled in knitting and crocheting. She didn't know then that her ability to use her hands to create would come into play in ways she could never have imagined.

\*\*\*

In 1961, we moved to Panama, near the Canal Zone. The climate was hot and humid, and if the weather didn't get to you, the mosquitoes would. My skinny legs, covered with scabs in different stages of healing.

My sister, Karen Marie, was born on March 14, 1962. I had just turned seven years old. My brother Eddie was two; only three months shy of his third birthday. It was a difficult pregnancy. My mother had to lie down with her legs elevated for months in order to increase Karen's chances of survival. Mom had several miscarriages prior to Karen's birth. Due to many female problems, Mom had to undergo a hysterectomy at some point after delivery.

My baby sister grew prettier with each day that passed. She had an olive complexion, dark brown eyes, and silky black hair. My mother would run her index finger along Karen's nose, admiring its defined bridge, a physical characteristic that Mom said Korean people considered attractive. She even put a clothespin on her nose to ensure it didn't spread wider.

Eddie and I loved to play with Karen, who would squirm in our little arms, futilely trying to regain her freedom. When she did escape, she would initiate a game of hide-and-seek. We could always find her because she couldn't control her giggles.

Eddie and I mischievously teased her about her Panamanian looks, telling her that her father was really a Panamanian—probably one of the dirty beggars we'd see when we visited Panama City. They squatted in front of storefronts wearing filthy, ragged clothes, their tin cups extended to passersby. Karen would cry uncontrollably until we reassured her that we were just kidding, and that she was really our sister, not a dirty beggar's child. Then she would smile and hug us.

Karen at age two years old

With another mouth to feed on an enlisted soldier's wages, my father took a part-time job in the evenings as a janitor. He worked for the Army during the day and came home to eat dinner with his family before leaving for his second job.

My mother also stayed busy. Taking care of her children and the household kept her occupied most of the day. She also used her tailoring talents to earn a few bucks sewing dresses for military wives.

The years of poverty had taught her to save money, and she hoarded every dime she earned from her small sewing business. She would send money to Korea to help her family or buy savings bonds, in each of her children's names, to save for our college fund.

My father was exhausted from his work schedule and constantly worried about making ends meet. In that frame of mind, he discovered that my mother was hiding her little stash of cash from him. His core values were trust and honesty, and Mom broke both. Ed, who struggled day and night to feed and clothe his family, found receipts for money order made payable to my Korean grandmother. This discovery prompted him to continue searching, which led him to the savings bonds in his children's names. My mother had earned more than three thousand dollars in 1962, valued at approximately twenty-thousand dollars in 2008, from her sideline seamstress work!

My father was outraged—not that she had helped her family or socked away money for her children's future, but rather that she didn't trust him. That she was capable of deceiving him.

How could he know that my mother could never truly trust anyone but herself?

***

Not only could Mom save money, she could make a dollar stretch. She would buy a pound of hamburger meat and feed a family of five on it for at least a week. Hamburger patties would be 5 percent beef and 95 percent breadcrumbs. Then there was her famous spaghetti sauce, into which she would deposit all of the leftovers from our meals at the end of the week. As children, we didn't know any better. We loved her cooking.

She also knew how to save money on clothing. She would find fabric on sale or buy bolts of cloth in large quantities at a lower cost. Out of that cloth, she would sew my brother a shirt, my sister a dress, me a dress, my Barbie doll a dress, and even herself a dress! She might even throw in a couple of pillow covers and some curtains, all out of the same fabric. Mom gave new meaning to the phrase *cut from the same cloth.*

My favorite fabric pattern was a navy blue flower on a white background. The flower looked like a sunflower with large leaves. I did feel sorry for my brother having to wear a shirt with a big sunflower pattern. Nevertheless, he seemed perfectly happy just to be wearing a new shirt.

When my mother finished sewing a new shirt or dress, we could wear it hot off the press. We were always excited to take a trip to Panama City to show off our new clothes, although the excitement was short-lived. I felt so sorry for the beggars squatting in front of the storefronts that I wished I had just worn my old clothes.

Our family would frequent the beach on the weekends. My mother grilled both hamburgers and hot dogs in the picnic area of the beach. We relished the barbecued food, starving after hours of battling the rough ocean waves on rafts. Sometimes Mom would join us on the raft. It was bit crowded, but we had a blast knocking around in the ocean. We were fearless, even as we gasped for air after swallowing what seemed like gallons and gallons of seawater. We stayed within the protective ocean fences meant to keep the sharks away from swimmers.

Frequently I had earaches after spending hours in the ocean. I would wake up crying in the middle of the night, and my father would pour salt into an Army sock, heat it up in the oven, and place it on my ear. The warmth seemed to make the pain go away. He had a way of making things right. He was my hero.

When we weren't at the beach, my brother, sister, and I played among the bamboo plants. We hid in the groves of overgrown bamboo, and made weapons, musical instruments, or whatever was our whim out of the sturdy stems.

While I have happy memories of living in Panama, it was also a strange period. I'm not certain why my mother acted so irrationally about nothing. I remember she seemed extremely irritable; her mood swings were unpredictable, seemingly triggered by nothing eventful. She would flare up at us for no apparent reason. I recall being afraid of going home after playing outside most of the day. I didn't know whether she'd be kind and mellow or if she would hit and scream at us. Later, I heard that she'd had malaria and suffered from high fevers and nervousness.

***

A couple of years later, my father again received orders from the Army and we relocated from Panama to Woodbridge, Virginia. It was the early 1960s.

We moved into a small, three-bedroom, one-story home on Melbourne Avenue. We bought a pink Rambler, which we parked in our carport. We had a nice-sized backyard and a chain link fence divided our and our neighbor's property. A few saplings landscaped our yard. Our home looked liked every other home in this middle-class suburb.

The neighborhood attracted many military families because it was affordable and the homes were new, as were the white sidewalks. Saplings lined the streets and schools were nearby. It was an ideal place in which to raise children.

However, it was not a very diverse neighborhood. I recall the residents looking alike: mainly white. I don't recall anyone, other than us, who looked Asian, Hispanic, or African American living in the neighborhood.

Our playground, a lake and forest behind the railroad tracks, was less than a block from our house. The railroad tracks divided our new development from undeveloped land. When I stood on the tracks and faced one way, I could see rows and rows of identical-looking homes. When I turned around and faced the other way, I could see open fields of overgrown weeds and a little forest beyond the fields, which we referred to as the "woods." The "woods" were a magical place, at least through my eyes, where fairies and goblins hid, a place where you could dream and fantasize about all kinds of things, like my contributions to humanity or the places I'd like to travel or the house I'd like to live in.

My brother and sister always wanted to tag along with me, and I tried to find ways to escape from them. I didn't want to babysit or have them running to my mother with tales. I just wanted to hang out with my friends or be by myself.

With little money, we had to find ways to entertain ourselves. We made a swing by tying one end of a rope to an old tire. Old fallen tree trunks served as a boat. Our flag was a white kerchief, tied to a branch sticking up from the log. One day we'd be pirates; the next, lost explorers.

The lake also dumped into a wide drain where the water cascaded to a sewer system, giving the appearance of a waterfall. We'd play in the "waterfall," not fearing drowning, snapping turtles, or water moccasins.

The woods beyond the railroad tracks sparkled in the winter with snow and ice. It was truly a winter wonderland. The tree branches looked liked crystal chandeliers, and we'd skate on the frozen creeks or just revel in their beauty.

In the warmer weather, the woods came alive with wildlife. You could hear noises of little creatures all around, but mainly they hid in the woods. I would lie down in the weeds that swayed gently in the breeze. With the warm sun blanketing every fiber of my body, I reveled in the calm of the moment.

When we weren't swimming in the lake or playing in the woods, we were playing in our backyard on our gym set.

At the end of the day, we'd look forward to dinner with the family. After dinner, my father would play with us, chasing us around the house or yard. Later in the evening, he could be seen at the stove, popping popcorn for a snack, or helping us with our homework.

We felt secure and happy.

\*\*\*

We were jolted from our comfortable life when Ed announced, in 1964, that he was going to serve military time in Vietnam. My mother was thirty-two, I was nine, my brother was five, and my sister was two years old.

My father was an electronics specialist and a sergeant in the U.S. Army. He was career military through and through, although he didn't fit the stereotype of being a harsh disciplinarian. He was kind, gentle, and quiet, not what you'd think of as the "military type." He was mild mannered, and he could always be depended on.

Before my dad departed for Vietnam, he made sure everything in the house was working properly. The bills were paid. The car was tuned. All repairs taken care of. Dad told me to assist Mom. He said, "Your mother will need you to read letters and pay the bills." He also told me to be a good girl, and that he knew he could count on me. I nodded in agreement.

My mother tried to put on a brave face, but I knew she was scared to death; being left in a foreign country where she had no close friends, a poor command of the language, and the sole responsibility of caring for three children. Ed was her lifeline. She had left our day-to-day existence in his capable hands; she didn't even know how to write checks or how to pay bills.

The dreaded day finally arrived, the day when Dad had to depart for Vietnam. When the time came for him to leave, we cried and hugged him, not wanting to let him go. His eyes filled with tears, and his nose turned red as he tried to hold back a flood of emotions. Not only would he miss us, he was concerned about how his family would cope without him. He was our rock. We were very dependent on him to take care of us.

\*\*\*

True to my dad's nature, he wrote to us every day from Vietnam. His letters meant everything to us.

"Mom, the mailman just delivered Dad's letter!" I would excitedly yell. That became our ritual. Since I was the eldest, I had the privilege of making that important announcement on days the mail was scheduled for delivery.

Then we would gather around the kitchen table. I would carefully open the letter so as not to tear the envelope. We wanted to keep everything intact and neat. I'd read his letter aloud to my captive audience. My mother would say, "Sujan, read that part again." So I'd read it again. If this occurred too often, I would get a little frustrated and say, "I already read it." Mom would respond, "If I could read English then I would do it myself!"

Dad would number each letter on the lower left side of the envelope, so I remember that he sent hundreds. As the numbers increased, we knew that we were getting closer to him returning home to us. Dad's letters always made us feel loved, as if he'd never really left us. He would remind us to pay the household bills. He would ask if we checked the oil in the car and the filters on the furnace. Had we bought our school supplies, were we studying, were we behaving?

Since my mother couldn't read or write English, I wrote the checks for the bills in my scrawled handwriting. I had to control my penmanship because if my letters were too big, I couldn't fit the writing in the space allowed.

Later, my father's letters hinted of something sinister. Vietnam was starting to change him. He didn't go into detail, but he'd give us small glimpses of his life in Vietnam: Pregnant women and their unborn children murdered. Vietnamese children butchered. Enemy heads stuck on tall poles. Blood, guts, and killing.

Dad wrote: War is not something I want my children to ever experience. If my time in Vietnam will prevent war in the United States, then it's worth it for me to stay as long as it takes. I guess he bought into the

Vietnam War propaganda. What other meaning could he have given this senseless conflict?

The United States' objective for involvement in the war was to prevent a communist takeover of South Vietnam as part of a wider strategy called containment. Despite the increasingly depressing news of the war, many Americans, such as my father, continued to believe the war was a noble cause because it would prevent a communist takeover of a pro-Western government in South Vietnam. Then there were the politicians who were more concerned about saving face in the event of disengaging from the war.

However, anti-war feelings also began to rise, as many Americans opposed the war on moral grounds that it was causing pointless deaths of both innocent Vietnamese civilians and American soldiers. In addition, many protested the conflict because they viewed it as a war against Vietnamese independence, or as the United States' intervention in a foreign civil war.

***

Eventually, Dad's letters began arriving less frequently. What started as daily letters turned into weekly ones.

That didn't deter me from looking for his letters every single day. I would check our mailbox several times a day, until a letter came or I knew it was past the mail delivery time. My father's letters defined our day. We were happy if we heard from him. On the days that we didn't get a letter from Dad, we'd be upset. We needed the stability and security those letters provided.

Each time we received a letter, we wondered if today was the day we'd hear the news we had been waiting for: the day Dad would return to us. We'd be a whole family again. We couldn't wait!

Today's letter was different. Inside the envelope was another envelope, addressed to my mother and written in Korean. This letter was off-limits to me. I handed it to her, and she held the envelope and gazed at it without expression. She slowly rose from the kitchen table and headed for her bedroom. Then she turned to us and said, "I go my bedroom to read your father's letter."

At first, I was hurt that Dad had broken our routine. We had undergone too much change; we wanted some semblance of normalcy. Then I chuckled as I concluded, *Dad wanted to write Mom a love letter. I guess that's okay.*

We three children stood outside my mother's bedroom door, anxiously waiting to hear when our father was returning to us. Three small ears pressed against our parents' bedroom door. There was no noise. Nothing. *When will she come out of the bedroom?*

*Wait a minute. Was that a muffled cry?* I became scared. *Had something happened to Dad?* I tried to put on a brave face for Eddie and Karen. Then my mother suddenly opened the door and we almost tumbled into her bedroom. Her eyes were downcast, and it looked like the blood had drained from her face. Now I knew: my father had been killed!

Mom slowly walked to an armchair in the living room. She looked sick; her face was pasty, withdrawn. The sides of her mouth turned down. There were so many tears; she didn't wipe them away. She didn't even seem to notice them. She just sat in the armchair and stared straight ahead while the tears streamed down her face, neck, and chest.

I was frightened. We couldn't take our eyes off our mother, but we were afraid to say anything. We knew something was really, really wrong.

Then my mother's head dropped forward like a limp doll. When she lifted it again, she also released a scream as primitive as a wounded animal. After this initial release, my mother started crying, her shoulders heaving. When she had no tears left, she stared at the living room ceiling, slowly sinking into the armchair.

My mother started kicking the coffee table in front of the armchair. Then, she began kicking harder and harder. The soles of her bare feet turned red first; then they swelled and turned a purplish color. She was too consumed in her own grief to notice the three small faces staring at her, three pairs of eyes also filling with tears. Three mouths open without words, wanting answers, but afraid to ask.

My mother mumbled quietly, "How am I going to take care my children? I never work. I cannot speak English. I cannot write English. I never work in the States."

When we learned the truth, it was worse than if I had heard that my father died. He'd fallen in love with a Vietnamese woman, with children from a previous marriage. He was leaving us to marry her and take care of her children as if they were his own. We had been replaced—like last year's clothing.

Now, this might not have come as such a surprise if it had been consistent with my father's character. But here was a man who, unlike many

American soldiers stationed in Korea, kept his promise to bring a young, vulnerable Korean woman and their baby to the United States. A man who would have rather died than not honor a commitment. A man who worked two jobs to support his growing family. A man who always paid his bills on time. A man who treated his wife as an equal. A man who made popcorn for and played horsey with his children. *Where did that loving, responsible man go?* Perhaps he really did die in Vietnam.

# CHAPTER 5

From that day forward, at the ripe old age of ten years old, I became the mother and father. I assumed the responsibility and the burden of my mother's pain, as well as mine. It was mine to bear because I could and I would. My father had no right to hurt my mother. I would make it better for her.

The world, as we knew it, had just ended. Our future, as we knew it, had just ended. Our lives, as we knew them, had just ended.

The horrors of Vietnam crept into our small home in Woodbridge, Virginia.

My mother remained slumped in the armchair for roughly a week, but it seemed like forever. I suppose she had to eat and go to the bathroom, but I didn't see her move. Her head was bowed, her body still, her breathing quiet. When the evening fell, shadows framed her despondent, vacant face.

As each day passed, I wasn't sure what the next day would bring. Would she ever get better? I couldn't depend on things ever being the same. At any moment, my whole life could change again. In an instant. With a snap of the fingers. Just like that.

The food and water I set on the table near Mom were untouched. The sun rose. The night fell. I tried to keep things as normal as possible for my brother and sister, fixing them breakfast and making sure we got off to school on time. I prepared our meals. I helped them with their homework. I put them in time-out when they needed to be punished.

My mother simply sat in her chair, all alone.

To her, we didn't exist. The world didn't exist.

She had no family to turn to.

No close friends to support her.

A sheltered housewife, all alone.

For a brief time in her life, she had felt that it was safe to trust and love. She should never let her guard down again. She should have kept hiding money from her American husband, like the stash of rice she'd hidden from Mr. Yeo. What seemed so long ago and a continent away came back full circle—feelings of betrayal, despair, sadness, and loneliness.

As my mother dealt with her pain, I dealt with my own.

Every time I started feeling sorry for myself, I thought, *Forget about it; I can't change what happened. Live with it. It is what it is. This is God's greater plan at work—one that I may never understand—but it doesn't matter because we are experiencing what we are supposed to be. I may never know the answer to "Why me?" but it doesn't matter. It's not for me to know.*

\*\*\*

Then, finally, my mother came alive. She stirred in the armchair that had held her captive for the past week and acknowledged us, her children.

She wasn't apologetic for being absent. She wasn't concerned about whether we'd eaten or attended school. Without asking, she knew that I'd taken care of everything.

My mother shook her head, as if awaking from a deep sleep. She looked different, like a woman with renewed purpose.

With conviction in her voice, she said, "What am I doing sitting here feeling sorry for myself? I have three children to feed. I have to work hard and give them a good education. I no depend on a man. I have to take care myself."

Koreans are like that. They want their children to have better lives than they themselves had. It's a generational thing: each generation should do better than the former. The path to achieving that goal is through education. Mom needed a purpose to live. Now, she recognized that she, and she alone, had to support us and keep our dreams of college diplomas alive.

My mother slowly rose from her chair. She shook her head again, as if to shake off the pain and hurt, and most of all, to shed her former life and start anew. It was time to move on and take care of business, the business of living and rearing her three young children.

But how? Where could she possibly start? What could she do?

There seemed to be so much going against her. No work experience. Illiteracy. Broken English. Few friends.

But don't underestimate the human spirit. My mother recognized early on that she was a survivor. And anything was possible if one wasn't afraid of a little hard work—and never, ever giving up. Her trust in something greater than herself allowed her to take risks. Her gratitude for the little things in life kept her positive about what lay ahead.

That type of spirit had gotten her to the bountiful and beautiful United States of America. My mother would say all the time, "Thank your daddy for bringing us to this country. This country is wonderful. All you need is two strong arms and legs, and you can be anything you want."

Although she was focused, positive, and ready to go to battle, the hurt and betrayal my mother felt never went away. I would see it rear its ugly head for years to come. It manifested itself in the form of cancer and a sadness that stained her eyes. She could never hide it from me. I saw it, even when she seemed happy to the rest of the world.

My mother lived with the hope that one day my father would return. She checked her mailbox every day for his letter, the one in which he professed that she was his true love, that he had made a terrible mistake in deserting his family. For fifteen years, my mother checked her mailbox, waiting for that damn letter. It never came.

I believe my mother would have forgiven him completely. Her loyalty to my father was unwavering. No one could say anything bad about him. She would tell us, "Your father, he good, kind man. He honest; he keep his promise and bring us to the United States. If we stayee in Korea, people treat you bad. They no like half-American children. They no give you education. They look down on you."

After that first week, her sadness worked in a strange way. It seemed to convert to energy. My mother would clean our home vigorously, always keeping herself busy, until exhaustion forced her to rest. She tried to save money by preparing meals that could stretch even further than before. She cooked large pots of beef soup, enough for an Army platoon. We'd eat that all week with white rice. Or, her famous spaghetti sauce would be bubbling on the stove, where all of the leftovers found a home.

We always seemed to have plenty of milk to drink. My mother would buy five gallons of milk a week from the commissary. She thought our military benefits couldn't be replaced—free medical, commissary, and the PX. She was eternally grateful to my father for them. But steak? What was that? A rare treat was to eat a hamburger and drink a milkshake at the local fast-food joint.

And we would never think of wasting electricity. Forty- and sixty-watt bulbs replaced hundred-watt bulbs. We turned off lights when we left a room. The heating/air conditioning unit ran at minimum comfort level. To me, it was good common sense that we shouldn't waste electricity. I never gave any thought to us having less than others. I loved my mother's cooking. I didn't miss sodas. When I was given a soft drink at a friend's home, it tasted yucky. I loved the taste of cold milk and fresh water. So what was there to miss?

After my mother tightened our family belt and reduced expenses as much as was practical, she focused on how she could earn a living. We couldn't depend on my father to send us money. He'd adopted a new family, and I for one no longer trusted that he'd do the right thing. Starvation would be a walk in the park compared to the hell he had put us through.

Mom asked her few Korean friends if they could help her find a job, any job. A couple of them worked as waitresses, and tips could be very good. Soon they hooked her up with their employer, and my mother went on her first job interview. Luckily, waiting on tables didn't require prior work experience. She was attractive, young, and healthy.

I anxiously waited to hear the news. I knew it meant so much for my mother to earn a living and support her family. I just wanted her to be happy. So I stood by the living room window, waiting for my mother's car to appear. As soon, I saw my mother's pink Rambler pulling into the driveway my heart started beating rapidly with anticipation. She jumped out and I ran out of the house to hear the news. "I have a job, I have a job, I workee!" she excitedly announced. We hugged and kissed.

My mother's new job as a cocktail waitress required that she drive about twenty miles, one way, from Woodbridge to Washington, DC. The hotspot was called the Butterfly Club. It was a topless nightclub, but the waitresses were, oddly enough, required to wear a pretty conservative uniform: a crisply pressed white blouse, a black skirt, a black apron, and black shoes. Perhaps it was a way to bring some degree of respectability to the club.

# CHAPTER 6

Shortly after my mother started her new job, she invited a male friend she'd met on the military base to our home. His name was Francisco Borego Garza, but almost everyone called him Frank. He was a stocky Mexican who probably didn't stand taller than five feet six. He had short-cropped black wavy hair, large dark eyes that drooped at the outer corners, long dark eyelashes, a big nose, and large ears. He used to be a boxer, and he looked like one. He was a mean-looking guy.

The minute I laid eyes on him, I didn't like him. I deliberately called him Sergeant Garza, so it would be perfectly clear that he had better keep his distance. I made it a point never to smile at him. In fact, in my mother's absence, I would scowl at him. I asked Mom why he had to be at our house, and she responded, "I feel better if someone is here with my children when I workee. He help me. He can read English."

Sergeant Garza brought us candy, his attempt to be nice and get on our good side. He didn't try to be our father. Without saying it, my mother was clearly in charge of her children.

But still, without being rude I made sure that he understood his place in relation to our family. He knew he wasn't welcome. Yes, he was Sergeant Garza. Not Frank. Not Mr. Garza. He would never be Dad. Not over my dead body. But I wouldn't have liked anyone that got too close to us. I didn't want another man hurting my mother.

My mother always said what was on her mind. She didn't believe in pretending. If she liked you, you knew it. If not, you knew it. She didn't pretend to be in love with Frank. She would state outright that she was still in love with my father, and would welcome him warmly whenever he decided to return. Meanwhile, Frank was her companion. He was strong and could help her with lifting heavy objects. He could read and write English, and keep an eye on her children when she went to work. But she knew better than to ever depend on a man for financial support.

Despite my mother's directedness, Frank was madly in love with her. He just wanted to be with my mother, on any terms possible. At a petite five feet one and 120 pounds, with black bouncy hair and beautiful skin, she was a head turner. He was not.

Frank didn't think it was safe for my mother to drive into DC at night, so he drove her to and from work. On occasion, we'd ride with them. I recall the first time he asked, "Do you kids want to come with me to take your mom to work?" We enthusiastically jumped in the car. We had never seen where she worked.

As we entered Washington, DC, we were fascinated by all of the tall buildings and city lights. As we got closer to my mother's place of work, we saw advertisements with nude women, surrounded by flashing neon lights, lining the fronts of nightclubs.

There were big burly men standing in front of the nightclubs' entrances, checking identification. Once in the club, these same men acted as "bouncers." If patrons were too rowdy, normally from drinking too much alcohol, they were literally bounced out of the club.

I curiously stared at a poster-sized billboard on the front door of the Butterfly Club, later renamed Benny's Rebel Room, where my mother worked. The small, round, blinking lights framing the billboard reminded me of Christmas. The poster had a picture of a stripper posing provocatively, her nipples covered with gold stars. Her other private parts were scantily covered with what looked like patches of cloth held together by string.

My mother saw me staring at the billboard and said, "Sujan, don't ever be ashamed of your mother. I lucky woman to have job." She pointed her finger toward the Butterfly Club. "I do what I have to do to support my children. Make better life for you. I don't do what bad girls do. I don't smoke. I don't drink. I don't go home with men. I just work, wait on tables. Make money, support my children. Please, you never be shame of your mother."

I nodded in agreement. I understood. She worked in a "sinful" place, but she was not sinful.

My mother was grateful that she had a job. And that is exactly what it was—a job. Unlike some of the other young women at the club, she went directly home when she finished work. She could have had a different date every night. But dating didn't fit in with her plans. She wasn't looking for a man to fulfill her life. After all, she was a married woman. She also had bigger plans than dating. She had the future of her three children in her hands.

Even so, waiting on tables wasn't easy. My mother's feet would swell from standing ten hours a day. By the time she pulled off her shoes, she would wince from the pain of her toes cramping. I would massage her feet. I recall how they felt like leather.

Despite the wear and tear on her body from the waitressing job, she remained ever so grateful to be able to work. She was especially pleased that her job allowed her to be with her children before and after school, when we needed her the most. While she was working, we were sound asleep in our beds.

*\*\**

One day, a woman from the Red Cross came to our home. Now I wonder if the woman was actually an employee of the county social services department and my mother only referred to her as a Red Cross worker. I heard my mother open the door in response to her gentle knock.

I peeked around the corner to see who our visitor was. We rarely had company, so my curiosity was piqued. What did this stranger want with my mother? Their voices were low, but I could hear what they were saying.

"A neighbor has asked me to investigate your living conditions," the woman said. "She said that you leave your children at home at night without adult supervision. We're concerned that they are too young to be left alone."

My mother yelled, "Sujan, come here!"

I entered the room. "Yes, Mom," I responded pensively.

My mother turned toward the Red Cross worker.

"My house is clean. My daughter, Sujan, takee good care of her brother and sister. She a good girl. She takee good care of them. I no trustee other people. They might beat my children. I have to work at night. I no have education. I have to work as a waitress. I'm a good mother. I not bad girl."

The Red Cross worker scanned the interior of our modest home. From where she was standing, she could see the living room, dining room, and kitchen. "You're right. Your house is so clean that you could eat off your floors," she said. "Well, I have to admit that your house is sure cleaner than the woman who complained. Do you mind if I talk with your daughter?"

My mom nodded.

"Hello, Susan," the kindly Red Cross worker said. "How old are you?"

I responded, "Ten." She seemed very nice. I liked talking with her.

"Tell me, what do you children do in the evening when your mother is working?"

"I cook our dinner. Then we wash the dinner dishes. Then we do our homework. Sometimes, we have time to watch TV or read a book. Then we take a bath. We brush our teeth every night. We're not allowed to leave our house or let anyone in when Mom's not home."

I didn't tell her about the time I was crawling around on the floor and a knitting needle pierced my big toe. I could feel the tip of the needle right under the skin on the other side of my toe. I hopped to a neighbor's home and asked her to pull the needle out of my toe. She asked where my mother was. Although I hadn't been instructed to lie, I knew my mother would get in trouble if I told the neighbor we were alone. So I told her that Mom would be returning from the store shortly.

The Red Cross worker seemed satisfied with my responses to her questions. She turned to my mother and said, "Your daughter is more mature than some eighteen-year-olds that I've met. It's hard to believe that she's only ten."

My mother beamed proudly. "She honest girl. I can depend on her."

I felt proud. I'd passed the test.

"I'll be back to try to help you," the nice Red Cross lady said. "Don't worry; no one is going to bother you again."

When she left, my mother was visibly upset. "They try to take my children. Why they want to make trouble? I just try to work hard. Why people have to be so nosey?"

At that moment, I hated nosey people. "Mind your own business and leave us alone!" I felt like yelling up and down our neighborhood. It turned out that my best friend's mother was the neighbor who had called the Red Cross. She was not a pleasant person. She was obese, and since she could not control how much she ate, she controlled her children's eating. I recall playing at my best friend's house when her mother wasn't home. My friend said we could eat a saltine cracker, but we had to be sure to clean up every crumb so her mother wouldn't know she had eaten.

The Red Cross lady did come back, but not in an official capacity. She and my mother became good friends. They had great respect for one another. They would talk and laugh. The Red Cross lady seemed surprised that my mother was capable of taking such good care of us with so little.

My mother liked her new friend. She didn't feel all alone, and she could depend on this woman to give her good advice, read a letter, or interpret a bill for her. Finally, she had someone to lean on that she really trusted.

Left to right: Susan, Eddie, Red Cross lady, and Karen

CHAPTER 7

My brother Eddie always seemed to be causing trouble, one way or another. Like the time he caught and killed a snake, the one animal that made my mother's skin crawl. She panicked if she even saw a picture of a snake. Eddie displayed the dead snake on a dinner plate and placed it right smack in the middle of the refrigerator. He arranged the snake's body in the shape of a rosebud donut.

He had seen my mother eating eel and thought that she might find the snake to be appetizing. Mom opened the refrigerator door, screamed bloody murder, and slammed the door shut. Then she chased my brother around the house, swatting him with a broom.

To make matters worse, Eddie lied, especially when he stole money from my mom. Lying was a deadly sin in our home. When my mother caught him lying, she'd hunt him down, leather belt dangling from her clenched fist. Her eyes would narrow, her brow furrowed, and the sides of her mouth turned down.

Even though he would lie and steal, I felt sorry for Eddie. I'd yell, "Run, Eddie, run! Hide, Eddie, hide!"

My brother would take off, diving under our pink Rambler and scooting his skinny body until he was under in the center of the car, well out of my mother's reach.

She would kneel on the asphalt driveway and peer sideways under the car, her head almost touching the driveway. She'd yell for him to come out. After about an hour, my brother tired of hiding and emerged to get his beating. Time never made my mother calm down. She was angrier than ever.

My sister and I would cry as my mother beat our brother unmercifully, shouting, "You lie to your mother. Why you lie? Why you lie?" Eddie would sob, saying repeatedly, "I'm sorry, Mom. I won't do it again. Please stop hitting me. I promise, I won't do it again!"

My sister and I would cry in unison, "Don't hit him! He's sorry!" We wished he would just be good, so we could have some peace in the house.

The woods, which served as my playground, now became my retreat, a place where I could escape and dream of happier times to come. As I had many times before, but with new meaning, I'd lie in my favorite place—the weeds—where I could hide from the world. Lying on my back, I would imagine flying in the clouds, zipping out of the cloud formations that looked liked human faces, buildings, and animals.

It was silent except for the sound of my breathing. Then I'd hear crickets in the tall grass and bird's wings fluttering in the bright sky. Butterflies would land on my flat chest. Just staring at the sky, arms limp at my sides, daydreaming of all the possibilities life could bring, I felt happy as the sun slowly warmed my face and body, just as it had many times before. That was something that couldn't be taken away from me.

We managed to resume a "normal" life. We built tree forts, skated, climbed trees, and rode bikes. Skinned knees were the norm. Our mother encouraged us to live life to the fullest, without fear. Her motto was, "If you don't feel pain or love, you may as well be dead."

I didn't miss having fancy new clothes, going on vacations, or eating out at nice restaurants. I thought I had it all. When you don't have it, you don't miss it.

Nevertheless, I had a father. I missed him.

## CHAPTER 8

"Mom, look what I found," Eddie said. He liked to rummage through trash cans, living the saying that one man's trash was another man's treasure. He handed my mother a real estate multiple listing for a home located in Arlington, Virginia. My mother couldn't read words, but she knew numbers. Ten thousand dollars for a bigger house—and close to Washington, DC. She was intrigued.

The next day she called the real estate agent who listed the property. A month later, we were packing our belongings and moving to Arlington, Virginia.

We children cried. We didn't want to leave our home. Dad wouldn't know where to find us if he came back, and we'd miss our friends. We didn't want to go to a new school. *What about the lake? What about the railroad tracks? What would we do in Arlington, Virginia?*

My mother didn't feel sorry for us. She didn't even seem sympathetic. So we didn't waste any more tears. She'd made up her mind—we were moving. My brother, sister, and I didn't have a vote. Mother knew best.

***

In 1967, three years after my father departed for Vietnam, we were standing in front of our new home. It was a two-story wood home with an enclosed front porch. The problem with the house was that it was downright ugly. It looked like a rotten banana with its skin peeled back. No wonder the county had condemned it. We were moving into a rotten, run-down house with peeling paint. We wanted to be back in our comfortable and new home.

My mother saw the house differently. It was beautiful—or it would be in the future. But I couldn't see past the present, and disappointment set in. Still, I knew there was no use complaining; I had to just accept that we were leaving our lake, our playground in the weeds beyond the railroad tracks, and all of our friends to move to this ugly, unwelcoming house.

I didn't think it possible, but the inside of the house was uglier than its exterior. Paint peeled back from the plaster walls; windowpanes were cracked and broken throughout—but we couldn't open the windows. They had been painted shut. The floors were warped from water damage, probably due to the leaking roof or broken plumbing pipes. The boiler that warmed the home's water and provided heating clanged when it started up.

We moved into the basement, the only livable space. It was musty. The walls were cinder block; the floor was concrete. Plumbing pipes and wiring were exposed across the ceiling and along the cinder-block walls.

Before we could begin repairing the house, we cleaned. And cleaned. And cleaned. I didn't think it would ever end. Broken glass, rusty nails, yellowing newspapers, and old broken bottles filled the rooms and hallways.

My mother would put away her waitress apron when she finished work, only to come home and put on an old pair of pants and a worn-out shirt. She would scrape, patch, and paint the walls, ceiling, and doors. The ceiling was the most challenging; she would climb a ladder and roll the paint on the ceiling until her arms ached.

I'm not certain how she learned these new skills, but she looked like a pro. Perhaps this is a stretch, but I guess the years of sewing and knitting provided her with some basic skills that she applied to carpentry, painting, and general home repair. That's the only explanation I could come up with as I watched her work and supervise her three young laborers. Frank didn't escape, either. She ordered him around too.

Her crew—her three children and Frank—scraped, patched, and painted the walls, ceilings, window frames, and baseboards. School was out, so let the fun begin! Our small shadows would dance on the newly painted walls as night fell. We would ask our mother, "When are we going to be finished working? We're tired. We're hungry. We want to play."

"We finish soon. Then we havee nice home. Just keep working," she replied.

She would sleep a couple of hours and then start the cycle all over again, only to be broken when she went to the Laundromat around two o'clock in the morning.

In approximately six months, the house was livable. The walls were vibrant with a fresh coat of paint, and pinkish aluminum siding covered the weathered wood shingles on the outside of the house. New windows allowed the house to breathe again. Water flowed freely in the pipes, not all over the floor. Lights worked. Voila!

\*\*\*

We couldn't wait to move upstairs. "Mom, I want the bigger bedroom facing the street," I said. "Mom, I want the bedroom next to Sue," my brother said. My sister was too young to care.

But Mom had other plans. "I spendee too much money fixing up this old house," she said. "I have to findee way for this house to makee some money."

The nice, sunny rooms upstairs soon filled with roomers. We resigned ourselves to making do in our tiny basement. Only mold thrived in that damp and dark space. Luckily, no one in our family was taller than five feet four, or we would have constantly hit our heads on the ceiling or the plumbing pipes.

Mom liked being a property owner. Compared to waiting on tables, collecting rent was a breeze. She would sit at the kitchen table and count her rent money. Then she'd count her tips from her job. Every penny was used for basics—food, housing, and last season's clothing. If there was any money left, it was promptly deposited into a savings account.

Still, she continued to work at night as a waitress, arriving home around two or three in the morning and sometimes going to the Laundromat while we slept. She didn't know what the heck she was doing, but she learned by doing. Something in her mind kept saying, *Keep going; this will be your way to educate your children. Keep going; don't stop.* So she kept going, year after year after year. It seemed that she never slept. She worked all day, painting, laying tile, and scraping roof shingles, anything to save a buck.

Once, I saw her sitting in her yard next to a pile of old bathroom tile. I asked her what she was doing. She said that she was scraping off the old grout and glue so she could reuse the tile. I couldn't believe it. I told her that it wasn't worth her time to do that, but she berated me for not appreciating the value of a dollar. After all, she exclaimed, the tiles were in perfectly good condition and could be reused in the future.

She hoarded everything! "You never know when you might need it," she'd say. We had tools, old sinks, doors, shutters, windows, used restaurant equipment, old wood, toilets, shower doors, and light fixtures stockpiled in every nook and cranny.

She even tried fixing a leaking pipe, but no matter what she attempted to do, she couldn't fix the leak. Finally, she had to break down and hire a plumber, but she intently watched him perform his task, using the opportunity to learn. Paying him for his services was painful. It set her savings back by one hundred dollars, which was like a million bucks to her.

\*\*\*

After successfully remodeling her first home, she caught the real estate bug. She wanted to do it again. She would sit on our front steps and stare at the house across the street, dreaming that one day she might be able to buy it.

But how? Where would she get the money? It was seemingly impossible for a woman on a server's salary, especially a single, foreign-born woman with a limited credit history and three children to support. How could she possibly think that she could afford a second home? No lender in his or her right mind would qualify her for a second mortgage, especially since the house would be used as rental property. So my mother decided that we'd move to the house. It would be our new residence, if she were lucky enough to qualify.

Meanwhile, more rooms meant more rent money, an extra fourteen dollars per week to put in her savings account. So while she was waiting to be approved for a second mortgage, she decided that she would add another bedroom to our house. The only space left was under the enclosed front porch. If the ground was dug, the new room could connect to the basement.

The problem was that there was dirt, rock, and plain old hard ground under the front porch. Well, that wasn't the real problem to my mother. The real problem was that she didn't want to have to pay laborers to dig dirt from under the porch to construct another bedroom.

The answer lay right in front of her nose. By then, Sergeant Garza had moved in with us. So my mother, at age thirty-five, had her ditch-digging crew: Sergeant Garza, Eddie at age eight, Karen at age five, and me at age twelve. There went our summer.

We worked seven days a week for roughly fourteen hours a day, with meal breaks. Social services would have had a field day with this information! And my mother was an early riser; by seven a.m. we were working. We'd finish around nine p.m. When my mother wanted a job completed, she was relentless. At the end of each day, my back would ache. She felt sorry for me, but she never said to stop working. Instead, she said, "We have to finishee, so we can pay our bills and my children can go to college."

We couldn't wait to return to school from our "summer break" to get a *real* break. We hauled hundreds of buckets of dirt and rock from where the hole was being dug and spread it out in the lower sections of the yard. Sometimes a bucket was so heavy it would require two of us to pick it up. Teamwork was pretty good, except when my brother disappeared.

Our tasks didn't allow time to play with our friends, so our friends would ask if they could help carry buckets of dirt. They thought it would be a great deal of fun, and of course, my mother willingly accepted any help she could get. In the beginning, our friends enthusiastically showed up every day. We'd have races to see who could carry the most buckets of dirt within fifteen minutes. Later, they grew tired of the "game," or perhaps their parents put a stop to it. After a couple of weeks, our friends stopped coming to our house, and we were back to the dull routine of carrying buckets of dirt and daydreaming of how much fun it would be to swim, play games, and laugh with our friends.

Finally, by the end of our school break, we finished digging a hole large enough to build a bedroom. Now it was time to frame the hole with walls. My mother purchased cinder blocks and bags of concrete, and we took turns stirring the concrete to a consistency that we thought might work. My mother was the "cinder-block mason." She spread a layer of concrete on the dirt. Then she laid a cinder block on the concrete. Everything looked good so far. She applied another layer of concrete on the cinder block. Then she began laying cinder blocks on top of the first layer.

Things didn't go so well from that point on. No matter how hard she tried, the cinder-block wall looked crooked—really crooked. After hours and hours of trying to build a cinder-block wall, she finally gave up and hired a brick mason who finished the walls in a day. She admiringly watched him, appreciating the ease with which he built the wall. She also used this opportunity to learn how to lay cinder block, just in case she needed to do it herself in the future.

After the walls were finished, Sergeant Garza used a sledgehammer to make a hole in the wall of the basement. We applied Build-Dry to the cinder-block walls with paint rollers and brushes. That would keep out moisture and water. Then we framed the cinder block with two-by-fours to hang drywall.

We had to hire an electrician to install the electrical wiring before we could begin hanging the drywall. Following the electrical installation, we nailed drywall to the frame. At first, we didn't know there was a special nail for drywall, so it seemed we were always having to redo our hard work. But that's how we learned: by making mistakes. It didn't even enter our minds to go to the library and learn from how-to books. If we'd known how much we actually didn't know, we would have been afraid to even begin.

I would help hold the drywall in place while my mother and Sergeant Garza nailed it to the wood frame. My brother, sister, and I would unload the drywall from the roof of my mother's car and carry it to the basement. We could only lift the drywall when we worked as a team. My sister and brother were shorter, so in order for them to help, I would initially lift the drywall so it was low enough for them to reach.

Last, the walls had to be finished. We'd apply drywall "mud" to the cracks and seams. My mother would tell us, "Be careful; don't apply too much mud. It is hard to sand." She also didn't want us wasting any materials—like drywall mud and sandpaper. After we finished sanding and vacuuming, we painted the walls.

My mother looked at the finished room admiringly. "With hard work, we can do anything." She was so proud of our accomplishments that she'd tear up.

Drywall dust and paint covered us from head to toe. I bet the neighbors felt sorry for us. We didn't see it the way it might have looked. Our leader—our mother—told us that we were lucky to be able to have a home, two strong arms, and two strong legs. So we felt lucky.

For years, my mother would periodically reminisce about our summer of digging out the room. She guiltily said that my back was probably injured because I had lifted so many heavy buckets filled with dirt and rocks. I tried to reassure her that it was okay, but another part of me was glad she felt guilty. I could use my back injury as an excuse not to work so hard whenever I wanted.

My mother was unstoppable. She drove others as hard as she drove herself. She just kept pushing at all costs. She seemed possessed by something stronger than herself.

# CHAPTER 9

We'd been living in our "new" old house less than two years. It was January 1969 and my mother was thirty-seven years old. Despite her youth, the physical labor required to repair the house started to have an effect on her health, and she was always tired. That was to be expected, since she slept only four hours a day, at most. Sometimes she'd work twenty-four-hour days, as though she was trying to run away from something. It was as if she thought that taking a break would find her in a dark hole, out of which she couldn't climb.

She would tell me that she grew so tired that she would fall asleep at work. Often, she sneaked to the bathroom, and in the privacy of a stall, she sat on the toilet and closed her heavy eyelids. Her friend, another waitress, would cover for her while she took these catnaps, but the nightclub manager soon suspected that my mother wasn't covering her section as she should. She was fearful that she'd be fired from her job.

Mom had known something was medically wrong with her for a while. She'd seen drops of blood on her underwear and knew it wasn't her normal menstrual flow, since she had a hysterectomy after giving birth to Karen. Yet, she wasn't alarmed until the spotting turned to a heavier blood flow. That, coupled with her extreme tiredness, prompted her to make an appointment to see a doctor at a military medical facility for tests. The lab results turned out positive for cervical cancer.

Mom was forced to quit her waitress job in order to get medical treatment, including radiation therapy. She was terrified not to have a job, although she was generating a little income from her rooming house. But mainly she was afraid for us. What would happen to us if she did not survive the cancer?

She needed to contact my father. She had managed to keep tabs on him through the military benefit application process. She asked my father to come to Arlington from California, his new residence since Vietnam, to stay in our home and take care of us while she was in the hospital. When he did not respond to her pleas for help, she contacted his commanding officer and made the same request. The CO forced my father to take care of us.

I hoped that this would be a turning point in our lives. I knew there must have been a good reason for my mother having cancer. At that moment, I felt God hadn't deserted us. Surely, when Dad saw us for the first time since leaving us, he'd love us again. Mom would get better, and we'd go back to being a "normal" family—a father, a mother, and children, who didn't have to dig ditches all summer.

My hope was short-lived. My father did not return. It was a stranger who looked like him and had the same name, the same face, the same nose, the same hair. But his hazel eyes were different. They no longer smiled and twinkled. They were vacant. Vacant of love. Vacant of kindness. Vacant of any parental connection.

My father stayed in a bedroom most of the day, barely talking to us. He treated us as if we were someone else's children and he was just the babysitter. It was very strange that this man, my father, could simply turn off his emotions. How could a father stop loving his children?

I noticed that he had changed his brand of cigarette. Knowing the answer, I asked him, "Didn't you smoke a different brand?" He denied changing brands. Even at my young age, I understood that to mean, *My past life doesn't exist.*

When my mother came home from the hospital, my father was already packed and ready to return to his other family—his only family, as far as he was concerned. I remember my mother stealing a letter from my father's things. It was a letter from my father to Hoa, his new wife. Mom asked me to read her the letter, and I reluctantly obeyed, feeling like a peeping Tom. And I didn't want to see my mother get upset by the contents of the letter, which was a love letter. My mother cried, and I felt sad and helpless. I couldn't change anything, no matter how hard I prayed and wished for things to be different.

My mother wanted to run. But to where? Korea is where she chose. She wanted to see her elderly mother before she died. Six months after my mother was diagnosed with cancer, she traveled to Korea, ahead of us, hoping to find housing before we arrived. We were to follow her in a month. I was completing junior high school and didn't want to leave the United States. But again, there was no reasoning with Mom. I had no choice but to take care of my brother and sister, leave the United States and my friends, and interrupt my schooling—all because my mother wanted to return to Korea.

Sergeant Garza was supposed to keep an eye on us. As far as I was concerned, he was simply a fly on the wall. In my mother's absence, I was in charge. And he knew it. I was all of one hundred pounds, compared to him at two-hundred-plus pounds.

My size and age certainly didn't exert any power over Mr. Garza. It was my unspoken knowledge. I knew he was messing around with one of the female roomers, a young blonde woman, and he knew I knew. We both knew I wouldn't tell as long as he didn't try to "parent" us. It was our secret, which worked out well for me. I didn't want to see my mother hurt again, and I certainly didn't want this two-timing cheater presiding over my siblings and me. Mr. Garza simply served his purpose: made my mom feel comfortable that an adult was taking care of us in her absence.

A month passed pretty quickly, and soon it was time for we children to travel to Korea. I remember how scary it was to board the plane and leave the United States with my little brother and sister in tow. Sergeant Garza waved good-bye to us from behind the floor-to-ceiling windows of the airport boarding area. He looked sad and teary-eyed. For a brief moment, I confused fear of the unknown with missing him.

I could barely hold back the tears. My chest was burning from restraining my emotions. I was frightened, but I couldn't show my fear. I had to be strong for Eddie and Karen.

Our flight to Korea required a stopover in Tokyo, Japan. The three of us held hands tightly as we walked on the airplane's plank. My mother had arranged for Red Cross workers to pick us up at the airport, but I was scared that no one would meet us when we arrived. Outside looked so dark. The airport was bustling with people—so many people—and not one familiar face.

Panic started setting in as we stood there among the sea of travelers. *Suppose no one came. Suppose we were standing at the wrong gate. Suppose no one could see us, three young children, among the crowd of adults.* The three of us just stood there, frozen, like a deer in headlights.

Finally, our "guardian angels" spotted us. I made eye contact with them as they worked their way through the crowd of people. They had kind faces. One of the Red Cross workers approached me, knelt down and asked me if my name was Susan.

"Yes," I said, with a sigh of relief. The Red Cross worker stood up and took my hand. The other Red Cross worker gently took my sister's and brother's hands. I could finally loosen my grip on them. A big weight lifted. It felt good not to be in charge.

A car whisked us to our destination in the dark of the night. I remember seeing construction and bright lights all around us. The Red Cross worker explained that road repairs took place in Japan at night or in the wee hours of the morning, since there was too much traffic during business hours. I was in awe because of all the lights, people, and congested streets so late at night. I couldn't imagine the place being busier during day.

The next day we boarded a plane for Korea. It seemed like an eternity, but we finally arrived at our destination. My mother and Korean relatives warmly greeted us at the arrival gate. We clung to our mother.

On the way to our new house, Mom said, "We have three rooms in the house. I buyee house for my mother. But we live there together until we go backee to the States." I thought, *Three bedrooms. That means we'll have to share a bedroom. Oh well, this is temporary.*

The cab pulled up to a home surrounded by a tall stone wall; we entered our property through an iron gate. The yard was very narrow, and the house looked very small as well. The window coverings were made of white rice paper. It looked like someone had glued together a hundred little wooden picture frames and glued paper to the frame.

We had to step up to a landing before entering the house. Before I could fully get inside, I was reprimanded by a short, hunched-over, ancient-looking woman. Her gray hair was tightly pulled back in a small bun, held in place by only a single chopstick.

My mother said, "You have to takee off your shoes before you go in house. Korean people thinkee shoe is dirty in the house. This is your grandmother. You bow to show respect."

I awkwardly bowed, then sat on the landing outside the house and removed my shoes. Inside the house were soft slippers that I put on.

My grandmother grinned and embraced us all. Tears flowed through the crevices and wrinkles on her face. She was happy to finally meet her American grandchildren. Looking around the house, I saw one room. Then I saw a second. But where was the rest of the house? I peeked into another doorway and saw what looked like the kitchen, though it seemed much lower than the rest of the house. *Hey, the tile floor is missing*, I realized. Was I seeing things? No. The floor was dirt. There was no refrigerator, no kitchen counter, no sink, and no stove with an oven. Where were the three bedrooms my mother had mentioned?

Curious, I found her and asked, "Mom, where are the three bed-rooms? Where's the bathroom? I thought you said this house has three bedrooms."

"I tell you three-room house. You see all of the rooms," Mom responded matter-of-factly. No guilt, no "I'm sorry I brought you here to this rat hole." Two rooms and a step-down kitchen with a dirt floor. One, two, three. "See, three rooms," Mom repeated.

"Where do we sleep? Where do we eat? Where is the refrigerator? Where do we go to the bathroom?" I asked anxiously. But I didn't dare show what I was really feeling: pure anger. That would have been disrespectful to my mother.

"We sleepee on these mats on the floor," she said, indicating with a nod of her head toward the mats neatly rolled up in a cupboard.

"Together? On the floor?" I asked.

"Yes; me, you, your harmony, Sumchum, Eddie, and Karen all sleepee in this room on the floor," she said. The English translation of *harmony* is grandmother and *sumchum* is uncle.

I was increasingly feeling unprepared and betrayed. "Who is Sum-chum?" I asked.

"He my brother. My brother, Mr. Yang," my mother said. "You know, I talkee about my brother, Mr. Yang."

Then she introduced us to the outhouse. What a joy to squat in the freezing cold weather to relieve ourselves. As usual, I did not think of complaining to my mother. She had been through enough without having to put up with my whining. I was trying to feel lucky, but it was hard.

"Where is the shower?" I asked.

"We go to bathhouse. Nice, hot bathhouse. Pay people little money to washee you," she replied.

*Great, now I have to go to a public bathhouse. Stand nude in front of everyone and be bathed by some stranger,* I thought. I didn't even like changing into a gym suit in front of the girls in my junior high school gym class.

"Oh," was all I could say. As in, *Oh no—I'm not putting up with this shit,* or *Oh brother, you've got to be kidding!* But I didn't say any of it. Just "Oh."

When I got past the culture shock, I had to look at the bright side of things, as my mother had taught us. So I tried hard to feel grateful. There was no furniture to dust. No refrigerator to clean. No kitchen floor to mop. No bathroom to scrub.

It was actually quite simple. I discovered we could do fine with much less. We'd start each morning by rolling up and putting away our sleeping gear—floor mats and blankets. Then we'd wash the floors with clean rags, on our hands and knees. Harmony was right alongside of us, singing Korean songs while she scrubbed the floor. Now I understood why we couldn't wear shoes in the house. The floor was our bed and where we sat to eat. It was surprisingly comfortable to sleep and sit on a clean, heated floor. The entire house was the size of just the kitchen and living room in our home in the United States. It was all that we needed to be comfortable.

When the floor was sparkling clean by Harmony's high housekeeping standards, we would set up a couple of small oriental tables. We placed red cushions on the floor around the table. These were our chairs. We were fascinated by the black lacquered tables, which were ornately inlaid with mother of pearl. The designs seemed to come to life: fiery dragons, *papa-sans* (old men) hunched over from years of carrying heavy buckets of water on their shoulders, ancient trees bent by the wind, swans floating among willows, snow-capped mountains, and bustling Korean villages. My brother, sister, and I would trace the outline of the figures with our fingers. That was our source of entertainment in the absence of a television set.

A local girl, plump and rosy cheeked, was happy to have a job as our cook. She would buy fresh fish and vegetables daily at the market, which was located right outside the gates of our home. For breakfast, she'd cook white rice and fish and prepare half a dozen or so pickled vegetables. There were no eggs or pancakes. But we weren't complaining. We loved eating Korean food at any time of the day.

Sometimes, there were times we'd miss eating American food—just a good old-fashioned American sandwich. A peanut butter and jelly sandwich would do just fine. We asked our housekeeper, but I guess our language barrier got in the way. She made us a fried egg sandwich with peanut butter and mayonnaise. Eddie, Karen, and I waited until our mother was out of sight, and then a food fight ensued. We certainly wouldn't eat an egg, peanut butter, and mayonnaise all mashed together between two slices of bread! The poor cook got the brunt of our frustration. She ended up with peanut butter on her face, mayonnaise in her hair, and egg all over her chest. Luckily, she was too good-natured to tattle on us.

The outhouse made all of us gag. We held our breath as long as possible when we had to go to the bathroom, but it was hard to hold your nose and balance yourself while squatting and wiping your behind and trying to make sure your pants didn't touch the damp ground—all at the same time.

We had heard horror stories of people falling into the "toilet" opening (which was a deep, dark, stinky hole) and drowning in their waste. We were extra careful when we had to use the outhouse to avoid that terrible fate.

In the winter, we tried to hold our urge to go as long as possible. If we did venture out in the cold, the bitter winter wind would nip at our privates before we could even go. By then, the urge was gone. But as soon as we'd snuggle in our fluffy comforter on the nice warm matted floors, the urge would return.

The outhouse was too much even for my mother to bear. She finally decided that we needed to go "high-tech" with the bathroom facilities. She had a flushing mechanism installed on a ceramic toilet bowl, mounted directly on the wood floor. We still had to squat over the ceramic bowl, but at least it wasn't over a dark, smelly, and seemingly bottomless pit. It was a hit in the village we lived in; people would stop by to flush the toilet. Then they'd place their hand over their mouth and giggle.

During the warmer months, our new toilet worked just fine. Still, outdoor plumbing in even a modified outhouse wasn't very efficient in the winter months. The pipes would freeze, and frozen water couldn't flush the waste. So we had to do our business in a can once the ceramic toilet bowl was full. Looking on the bright side of things, at least the freezing temperatures kept the smell at a manageable level.

Few homes, if any (at least in our village), had a refrigerator, but there really wasn't a need. People shopped the open market for fresh meat and vegetables every day. In addition, the market served as a place for Koreans to exchange pleasantries and gossip. There wasn't much else to do to break up the routine other than eat, sleep, and yes—use the outhouse.

You would have thought, then, from the reaction and stares of our neighbors, that the Pope was visiting us when our new refrigerator arrived. My mother purchased it from the PX on a military base. Now we could have a glass of cold milk whenever we wanted it. We'd never paid a bit of attention to our refrigerator in the U.S., but in Korea, we revered it as if it were a prized calf.

## CHAPTER 10

I was enrolled in the ninth grade at the American school located on the military base. That's where I met Wendy. At five foot three, she was an attractive blue-eyed blonde. We instantly became best friends.

I was painfully shy. Wendy was the complete opposite. She and her friends would stand around smoking cigarettes before and after school. Although I'd never tried smoking, I wanted to fit in. At first I gagged, but then I got the hang of it. It was pretty cool to smoke, and if I smoked, I didn't have to carry on much of a conversation. I could just hang out and listen.

My mother would have killed me if she'd found out I smoked. According to my mother, Korean prostitutes smoked, not good girls. But I figured I'd give them up after I returned to the United States. Besides, she was the one who had made me come to Korea!

Wendy's father was a colonel in the U.S. Army and her mother was a stay-at-home mom. They were my idea of perfect parents: kind and undemanding. They encouraged us to have fun and enjoy the life of normal teens.

Wendy had a sister named Dani. Although they were very close, I recall Dani and Wendy arguing quite loudly. One time, I bought a blouse at the PX that was the same as Dani's. It wasn't like there were a lot of clothing choices on the military base. Dani told me not to wear mine because she didn't want us wearing the same blouse. "And besides," she said, "you are so flat-chested that you wouldn't look as good as I do in it." I was hurt by that comment, and Wendy came to my defense by going after her sister with two clenched fists.

Although I was horrified that I was the cause of the sisters fighting, I also felt even closer to Wendy, since she took my side over her sister's side. In fact, we became so close that we decided to be blood sisters. We both cut our wrists just enough to produce a small amount of blood. We sealed our friendship by rubbing our wrists together.

Wendy's parents were very happy that Wendy had such a close friend. They invited me to stay in their home, and I was more than glad to accept. They had real American furniture and accommodations: bunk beds and a regular toilet that you could sit on. They even gave me an allowance every week. I grew quite fond of Wendy's family.

Wendy hung out with an all-male Korean band called the He Five. They sang Beatles songs in perfect English. Otherwise, they couldn't speak a lick of it. Wendy could speak enough Korean to communicate with them, while I looked Korean, yet couldn't speak the language. So she served as an interpreter between the band and me—and Korean taxi drivers and me and Korean retailers and me. I was embarrassed that she had to interpret my native language for me, so I would pretend I was a deaf-mute in those situations.

The He Five would play at nightclubs. Wendy and I were their fan club. We followed them from club to club, cheering them on. The He Five also appeared on a local Korean television program and asked Wendy to be their backup dancer. She agreed, as long as I was included. The band had no choice; if they wanted Wendy to dance, I was part of the deal.

Wendy and I designed our stage costumes. We selected aquamarine material for our pants, which were bell-bottoms with slits on the sides of the leg that went a quarter of the way up the side. The pant slit was covered in white, brocade material that looked like it could have been used to make curtains. A little white button was sewn on the top of the slit. When the Korean tailor finished sewing our pants, we just screamed with joy. We loved our new costumes and couldn't wait to appear on television.

There was one problem: I had no rhythm. I tried to keep up with Wendy, who was a marvelous dancer, but when she stepped to the left, I stepped to the right. Wendy tried to cover for me, telling me to just watch her and stay in step. The He Five saw right through our ruse. They knew I couldn't dance. But they had no choice because Wendy, once again, came to my defense. She was my loyal friend. If they didn't want me, then she wouldn't dance for them. She was the one they wanted because of her Caucasian looks and her dancing, so to keep her, the He Five resigned themselves that I would be one of their backup dancers.

I became somewhat of a celebrity in the little village where we lived. My brother would make fun of me. Eddie said that he'd seen me on a television in one of the storefronts. He would point his finger at me and start swaying back and forth. "Susan, you looked like a jerk," he would laugh. I just pretended his comments didn't bother me, but I knew he was right. I did look like a jerk.

Wendy and I were always busy exploring Korea together. We'd eat steamed dumplings and marinated beef at restaurants, and drink Singapore slings at local bars. I guess the drinking age restrictions were loose in Korea. We'd enter singing contests, although my singing ability wasn't any better than my dancing ability. We'd travel with the He Five to their gigs and go to school dances on the military base. I decided I could get used to living in Korea, as long as I had my pal Wendy by my side.

But things suddenly took a turn for the worse. I'm not sure how I heard the news. Somehow, Wendy's father knew. My mother was in trouble—she was locked up in a Korean jail for selling merchandise on the black market. The goods looked innocent enough—white pumps and matching purses. My mother, a criminal. And to hear the news from—of all people—Wendy's father, a high ranking officer in the Army! Would my life ever be normal? Embarrased, horrified, angry, frightened—doesn't begin to describe the range of emotions I felt.

I remember the black-and-white photo of my mother taken by the police after they arrested her. She looks forlorn and beaten down. She is sitting on the ground in front of a mound of merchandise wrapped in paper that she bought in Japan. Someone must have convinced her that this would be a lucrative business. She was naïve in that way.

Picture taken by Korean Police of Moon Ja

We had to leave Korea immediately. Somehow, Wendy's father pulled some strings and managed to get us out of the country on a medical military airplane. I believe he was able to do it because my mother was in need of medical attention. She still needed medical care for her cancer.

Just as I had left the United States, less than a year earlier, with my stomach tied in knots, so I returned. I would miss Korea. I would miss Wendy and her family. Just when I had settled down in Korea and was happy, I had to uproot and leave my new best friend and my kind, new, normal family. A family that had a mother and father who loved one another. A family life where there was no drama. No houses to paint. No ditches to dig.

I felt like I had to start all over when I returned and went to a new high school in the United States. I felt like an outsider. I was addicted to cigarettes. My former friends gagged when I lit up. School dances and hanging out at McDonald's were boring compared to my life in Korea, where we went to nightclubs, bargained at the open markets, sang, danced, and were free.

I no longer fit in with my high school friends in Arlington. So I came to admire a new group of friends, called hippies. At the same time, I wasn't willing to lose my old friends. So I straddled two worlds, hippies and cliques. The former was risky; the latter was conservative. My needs were met—adventure and security.

## CHAPTER 11

We quickly picked up where we had left off before going to Korea. My mother's cancer went into remission after she underwent more medical treatments. She really didn't discuss it much; instead, she treated it as if were a non-event. She set the tone for where illness fell in the list of crises for the rest of the family. Being naïve about cancer, I didn't realize that she had silently endured a life-threatening, painful disease.

Knowing what I know now, I realize Mom wouldn't have seen any point in worrying her children. How would that have helped her get better? She chose to live as if she were cancer free, acknowledging that when it was her time to die, there was nothing she could do to change it. It was in God's hands. All she could control were her attitude and her actions, so she chose to stay as positive as possible and work as hard as her body would allow.

My mother returned to her waitress job, but her real love was fixing up old houses. It brought out all of her creativity. She could work all night doing it. Although she still couldn't read or write English, she had an instinct for real estate. She was confident that property would be her ticket to achieving her dreams: a college education for her children and helping her Korean family live a better life. Property was solid. She could see it and feel it. It was a moneymaker.

In 1970, the same year we returned from Korea, Mom tried to buy a second home—the one located across the street from our home, the one she had dreamed she would own one day. The same questions haunted her. As a single mother on a waitress's salary, how could she possibly qualify for a second home?

My mother respected her former settlement attorney and considered him a friend. She assumed that anyone with a college degree had all the answers. Since the kindly settlement attorney was an educated man, surely he could help my mother find a way to buy another home.

Mom told me that the settlement attorney visited our home and was shocked that my mother and three young children had performed such miracles on an old, dilapidated house. He was so impressed with my mother's tenacity and work ethic that he found a way for her to qualify to buy the house across the street. He lent her part of the eighteen thousand dollars needed to purchase it.

Little did Mom know that she'd bought a second good investment. She'd prove to have a knack for buying rundown homes in neighborhoods where real estate prices would go through the roof decades later.

Now that we had two homes, my mother officially became a real estate investor, property manager, and landlord. She'd sit at the kitchen table calculating her new mortgage and utility payments, and how much rent money the homes could generate. She taught herself how to create a budget, without knowing the term for what she had accomplished, using her instinct.

The condition of my mother's latest purchase was rundown, although not condemned like our first Arlington home. Five male medical interns had lived in the house, and they must have not used a wastebasket to dispose of their college and residence papers. I've never seen so many papers! Every square inch of floor space was covered with about two feet of paper.

Having gone through this once, I knew what was in store for us: more cleaning, scraping, and painting. No summer breaks. No social time. Work, work, and more work. My mother didn't coin the phrase "Time is money," but she surely lived it. She never expected others to work harder than she did, but her work schedule was hard to match.

At least Eddie, Karen, and I slept at least eight hours a day. Mom certainly didn't want to interfere with our ability to do well in school. I recall many days that she worked around the clock until she could no longer stand. Her feet would swell to the point where she would have to slit the sides of her work shoes. Her leg muscles involuntarily convulsed until she would cry out in pain. My mother would say, "My leg muscles are twisting." I would try to stop the pain by massaging her legs and feet.

If her body hadn't forced her to stop, she would have just kept going. Her aggressive timelines were in line with the mortgage payment due date. If we could move into our new home soon, she could rent more rooms in the house we would be vacating. However, Sergeant Garza wasn't able to help repair the properties as much as he had in the past. A few months earlier, he had suffered a heart attack.

His first symptom was sweating, then pressure, like an elephant sitting on his chest. We called 911. When the paramedics arrived, they had difficulty carrying his heavy body out of the narrow stairwell leading to our basement. To my horror, there were a few instances where it appeared they would drop him. I felt like I was standing on the sidelines of a race. If they made it over the door's threshold, they were winners.

After this incident, I began calling him Frank rather than Sergeant Garza. He looked weak after his heart attack. Whatever ill feelings I harbored lost their significance.

***

It seemed forever, but it was only thirty days before we moved to our new home across the street. There was still much work to do, but it was livable.

Shortly after moving into our new home, Mom was in a car accident. She sideswiped the 14th Street Bridge's guardrail, smashing the passenger side of the car. She was driving home from work around two a.m. Overcome with sleepiness, she fell asleep while driving, an increasingly more frequent occurrence. Her white blouse bloodied from the gaping wounds on her injured head and nose. She said her arm felt like it was broke. As I looked at the car's damage, I was in disbelief that the car was drivable. Frank took her to the emergency room to treat her wounds. The emergency room physician was concerned she may have suffered a concussion. The next day she returned home. She was so bruised and sore, her recovery required bed rest for at least a week.

Later, she told me that she believed someone was looking out for her. Just as her car was about to hit the bridge's wall, she jerked the steering wheel in the opposite direction. She didn't turn the wheel fast enough to avoid hitting the bridge. Nevertheless, she escaped death, which she believed would have been her fate if something hadn't tapped her on her shoulder, awakening her just in the nick of time.

Soon after Mom recovered, she didn't waste any time renting every square inch of our former home. She even erected walls and a door to the enclosed front porch. Another bedroom meant more rent money. More money meant my mother could buy yet another home. Another home meant more money to buy another home. It seemed to be an endless loop. The headaches associated with managing tenants (rooming house tenants were a special breed unto themselves) didn't seem to bother her. It was part of the job she created for herself.

There was a glitch, however. My mother wasn't certain whether the county property zoning would allow her to operate a rooming house. According to her calculations, renting rooms was much more lucrative than renting the entire house to one family. When she asked, the county said that the house had operated as a rooming house long before the area was zoned for single-family homes, so it had been grandfathered as a rooming house. But when we moved in and used it as a single-family house, it lost its boarding home exemption. Mom didn't see how she could meet her mortgage payments and fulfill her objectives for her family if she didn't continue to operate the home as a rooming house. So she didn't comply with the county zoning regulations.

Routinely, a county inspector would conduct an inspection of the use of the house. The inspections were usually triggered by a neighbor or a disgruntled tenant, but the inspectors seemed to be sympathetic toward my mother. They saw how hard she worked. She could be seen painting the house, cleaning the yard, planting flowers. The inspectors would slap her with a violation notice, but then they would quietly disappear. They knew that she had single-handedly, with the help of her small crew, greatly improved the condition of the formerly condemned house. If anything, she contributed toward improving the neighborhood, a task few people had the backbone to undertake, much less an illiterate single mother of three.

In the meantime, my mother lived in fear every single day. She would worry and fret about the county evicting her tenants, which would cause her to lose her stream of income. She became so concerned about hearing bad news from the county inspectors that when the phone or doorbell rang, her heart would beat faster. The doctor told her that she was suffering from anxiety attacks.

I would have been thrilled if the county had forced my mother to rent to a single family. If we couldn't rent rooms, I wouldn't have to clean them every week. I had to change and wash the sheets, dust, and vacuum the rooms. Of course, it had to be done on Saturday, the day all of my friends would be shopping, riding around in cars, and having a good time.

My mother preferred to rent to men. "Women too fussy, complain too much, makee too much trouble," she would tell me when a female inquired about renting a room. She also didn't want to chance a mattress being accidentally stained with blood during someone's monthly period.

I hated cleaning the rooms, but I would never have thought of complaining to my mother. I would perform this dreadful chore week after week after week. In general, the rooms smelled like stale cigarettes, smelly feet, and body odor. A memorable room was the one occupied by a short Italian barber. His room smelled especially bad. It smelled like his black hair looked—greasy—mixed with hair tonic and cheap cologne.

I felt as though I were invading the roomers' privacy. They would leave girlie magazines strewn around, along with their dirty socks and underwear. I'd bring along a yardstick to pick up their personal items. I wasn't going to chance catching cooties by handling their intimate articles of clothing.

Usually, I was fearful that a tenant would return while I was vacuuming, so I frequently would turn off the vacuum cleaner to listen for footsteps. If I didn't hear anything, I'd continue vacuuming. Then I would change the sheets. It was hard to figure out if the sheets were full or queen size; they had been washed so much that the size had faded from the labels, and most times, I couldn't tell until I had already tucked in a side under a corner of the mattress. I'd try to stretch the sheet to tuck in the other side and it wouldn't fit. Sometimes, it would take two to three attempts before I got it right. Daylight was escaping, and I wanted to finish quickly so I could meet my friends.

Within a year, my mother changed her business model. She decided that the tenants could take care of themselves, and we cut out the cleaning service. What a relief! I'd found my ticket to freedom. I should have known that my freedom would be short-lived.

In August 1971, my mother bought another home that fit her investment profile: big, old, rundown, and a "good deal." We referred to each home by its address. This one was called I East Luray Avenue. My mother had just turned thirty-nine in July. I was sixteen, my brother was twelve, and my sister was nine.

Back to the same routine: clean, scrape, and paint.

***

As a sophomore in high school, I became increasingly aware of how unfashionable I was. My friends dressed in the latest clothing, and their shoes and purses looked modern. My clothing and accessories were obviously from last season's sales rack, if I was lucky. I decided I needed to earn some discretionary money, knowing that my mother would still expect me to work at fixing up old houses for the greater cause: my future education.

My first job was at Hecht's Department Store. I worked as a waitress in a restaurant located in the basement. It turned out I hadn't inherited my mother's waitressing skills. I lacked the ability to recognize faces, so I would be confused as to who had ordered what. I'd wander from table to table asking, "Did you order a cheeseburger?" Or I would serve ice cream before the customer was halfway through the main meal.

I'd search under the plates for a tip, but in most cases, patrons didn't leave one. I should have taken the hint and quit, but I kept going. At least I could depend on receiving my wages. Sixty-five cents per hour wasn't much, but it was better than nothing. Occasionally, a sympathetic friend who ate in the restaurant would leave a buck or two.

My tiny frame looked ridiculous in the oversized waitress uniform. My flat chest couldn't begin to fill in the uniform's darted top, and the skirt hung to my feet. I wasn't allowed to cut the dress to properly hem it, so the hem was turned under at least five times, creating a bulge about four inches thick at my knees. We were required to wear hairnets, as well, which I placed over my long ponytail.

That job was short-lived, but it was not of my doing. One day, my boss called my home to see if I could work an earlier shift, and my mother answered the phone call. She told my boss that he didn't pay me enough for me to continue working there. And, she asked, what was he thinking, trying to make people work so hard for nothing? She ended by telling him the restaurant was a terrible place to work because it didn't even have customers who tipped. She forgot to tell me about the phone call. Basically, on my behalf, my mother threatened my boss—pay me more or I would quit.

I arrived to work at my usual time, and my boss looked at me in surprise. He asked me to meet him in his tiny office. He seemed irritated with me. Straight out, he told me to turn in my uniform and leave. He said that he didn't appreciate being yelled at by my mother, and that if I thought I could earn more then I should do just that. I tried to explain that when my mother got excited her voice grew loud, but he didn't want to hear anything further. I was terribly embarrassed. I quickly changed back into my clothes, returned my uniform, and bolted from the restaurant.

I needed to find another job if I hoped to buy more fashionable clothes and a car. Mom told me that her friend had an opening at a local dry cleaners and phoned to see if she still needed someone. She told me to go straight to the dry cleaners because I was needed immediately. My mother pointed toward the direction of the dry cleaners, which she said was located right up the street on Pershing Drive.

I quickly walked to the dry cleaners and asked for the manager when I arrived. The man looked irritated that I was bothering him.

"Hi, my mother told me to come here because you want me to begin working right away."

The dry cleaning manager looked at me as if I were crazy.

I tried to clarify. "My mother, Moon, you know Moon. You were just on the phone with her, less than twenty minutes ago."

"No, I don't know anyone named Moon."

I couldn't believe it. She'd done it again! Couldn't she get anything right? I was very embarrassed that I had bothered this busy person. I sounded like a real live nutcase. He'd probably never heard of a person with a weird name like Moon. He probably thought I was some kind of prankster. I wanted to quietly slither out of the dry cleaners.

To my surprise, the dry cleaning manager said, "I don't know a person named Moon, but I do need some help. You can start next Monday." It turned out I would be earning a whole dollar more per hour than at my former job. I was thrilled—a real job.

A couple weeks after I started my new job, I was promoted to night manager. It was by title and responsibility only; I wasn't paid a dime more, but I didn't care. I loved the additional responsibility. I also liked being trusted. I reconciled the cash register, made bank deposits, and supervised one other part-time employee, a soldier in the Army.

He was funny, and we would go out together as friends. He would ask me to go with him to visit his boyfriend, so his boyfriend wouldn't "jump his bones" when he just wasn't in the mood.

When the cash register came up short a couple of times, however, there was no question who had stolen the money. My gay soldier friend's employment was terminated.

I eventually managed to save enough money to buy the clothes I longed for, and a used car. I pushed the car more than I drove it; it was always breaking down in the most inconvenient of places. But I loved that car.

The dry cleaning job not only gave me a means to meet some of my material goals, but I also learned an important lesson, among many. When

I complained to my mother that customers' clothes stunk, instead of sympathizing with me, she harshly reprimanded me. "Sujan, if their clothes smell good, then you don't have job. What do you expect if you work at dry cleaners—clean, fresh-smelling clothes? Whatza the matter with your thinking?"

To this day, if I even think of complaining about my job, I immediately recall her words. My whole attitude changes from one of complaining to one of being grateful for what I have.

CHAPTER 12

In 1972, during my sophomore year in high school, my mother was successful in bringing her number four sister and family to the United States. She was happier than I had ever seen her.

My aunt, uncle, and four cousins moved into our home. Their eldest daughter and I were the same age. They couldn't speak English, and they would live with us until they could find jobs and homes.

Within the next few years, Mom brought her mother (harmony), all of her sisters, her brother, and their families to the States. My mother even sponsored two Korean families who were not blood relatives. She learned of their desire to immigrate to the U.S. when she was a member of The Korean Wives Club. We counted that she was responsible for hundreds of Koreans immigrating to the U.S. We'd laugh when we would read in the newspapers that the Korean population was increasing in Arlington.

It was the same routine when my newly immigrated Korean family arrived to the United States. They would stay at our house until they could find jobs and housing, except one, my Korean grandfather. It's ironic that Mom's deceased father's (*who had too much pride to graciously accept desperately needed American money and disowned my mother for marrying an American*) ashes were flown from his burial site in Korea to his final resting place—America. Revenge is sweet! As amusing the thought, that was not my mother's motive. She didn't want to leave her father (albeit ashes) in Korea absent immediate family members, especially Harmony, who visited and ceremoniously honored his grave when she lived in Korea.

I felt put out of my own home. I was tired of living in crowded, close living space and hearing the constant Korean chatter, which was annoying because I couldn't understand a word of it. I was weary of my mother asking me to complete all the paperwork for her family, including immigration-related documents, rental applications, job applications, and school applications.

My mother called everyone she knew to try to find them jobs—and even people she didn't know. She didn't mind pulling up to a fast-food drive-through and asking the server if there were any job openings for her family, although they couldn't speak English. They eventually landed low-paying jobs with local Korean businesses, carry-outs, and such.

I would wonder, *How is that big family going to survive on so little money?* But indeed, they did survive, and eventually bought their own businesses. They succeeded because the whole family pooled their paychecks. It wasn't merely the parents' responsibility to take care of the family. Every working-age family member deposited his or her paycheck into the family bank account. The matriarch of the family managed the money.

The children didn't whine about wanting cars, new clothes, or money for dates. When the children received their paychecks, they gladly handed them over to their mother. These "family funds" supported their day-to-day existence, and what remained was saved. Vacations and expensive dinners would come later, after taking care of the basics. Buying a business, then a home—in that order—was the priority.

Even when my Korean cousins married and moved out of their parents' homes, they remained responsible for financially supporting their parents.

Although I admired my Korean families' hard work ethic and values, I didn't embrace them. I was uncomfortable being in public with them. I was painfully shy and only wanted to fit in. When I was with my Korean family, I felt like everyone was staring us. They looked different, spoke a foreign language, and behaved differently. Although, in reality, I looked like them.

I couldn't talk to them, and they smelled like garlic; their dress and mannerisms were so—foreign. I was ashamed of my feelings of not wanting to be seen in public with my relatives. Or perhaps, the real reason for my discomfort is that I didn't want my difference magnified by their presence.

Since I could communicate in English, I would take my newly immigrated Korean family to various appointments. One instance really stands out: I took my grandmother to her doctor's appointment. I dreaded having to inform yet another person that I couldn't speak a word of Korean when, by all appearances, I should have been fluent.

Top, left to right, top row: Moon Ja's sisters; lower row:
Moon Ja's brother, Harmony, and eldest sister
Lower, left to right: Eddie, Karen, Moon Ja, and Susan

Harmony looked even older than when I saw her last in Korea. Her hair had turned completely gray, though she still wore it in a tight bun. She resembled an elderly Native American. She could even pass for a male. She was only sixty-nine, but she looked to be a hundred. Her hard life had taken its toll.

As Harmony and I walked toward the medical office's entrance, she placed her hand over her nose and blew very loudly into her hand. I was shocked. But there was no stopping her. She shook her hand toward the ground, mucus flying everywhere, and then wiped the remaining mucus from her hand with a tissue. She safely tucked the used tissue back in her pocket for future use.

I looked around. Had anyone witnessed the barbaric act? I felt like the entire world was looking at us. I took Harmony by her elbow to steer her toward the medical office's entrance, as quickly as her short, stiff legs could move.

Finally, we arrived at her physician's office. Now, I thought, we were safe. I motioned for Harmony to sit on a chair while we waited for her name to be called by the receptionist. But like my mother, Harmony had a mind of her own. She walked to the desk and stood in front of the receptionist. As soon as the woman acknowledged her presence, Harmony slowly pulled a brown paper bag out of her shoulder bag and set it on the desk. Then she pulled a clear glass gallon jar from the brown bag—a former kimchee jar. (kimchee is a Korean staple. It is a fermented, smelly spicy cabbage loaded with garlic, scallions, hot pepper, salt, and ginger.) There sat the gallon jar in plain sight, for everyone to see, containing Harmony's stool sample. Whoever heard of bringing a gallon's worth of crap?

The receptionist tried to muffle her laughter while I quickly shoved the jar into the paper bag before other patients noticed it. Luckily, most of them were reading or sleeping. I simply wanted to crawl out of that office, and silently cursed my mother for putting me in another embarrassing situation.

If that wasn't bad enough, when I motioned for my grandmother to sit in a chair, she squatted on the floor in the middle of the waiting room. I tried to pull her up by the elbows, but she stubbornly refused. I'd pull her up, and she'd plop right back down into a squatting position. Finally, I gave up. I sat on the chair in the waiting room, thinking, *It will only be a few more minutes before the doctor sees her. Then I can get out of here.*

In the meantime, a new patient had arrived. She looked at me. She looked at my grandmother. Being the only two Asians in the room, it wasn't difficult to assume we might be related. The woman looked back at me as if to say, "What are you doing sitting in that chair while your grandmother is sitting on the floor?" She tried to help Harmony stand up, but my grandmother plopped right back down into her squat. I explained to the Good Samaritan that my grandmother had arrived recently from Korea and that she preferred to squat on the floor rather than sit in a chair. The woman just shook her head in disbelief or disgust.

CHAPTER 13

The year 1972 not only marked my Korean families' immigration to the United States, it also was the year I met my future husband. My life after high school graduation was all set. I'd been accepted to Radford University, an all-female college at the time. My college roommate was a friend I'd known in high school.

I met Victor at a high school hangout. Sophomores, juniors, and seniors from a couple of local high schools would meet at a club in Washington, DC, The Campus Club, located near George Washington University. To enter the club, you had to be eighteen years old. At the time, driver's licenses were made of plastic with raised letters and numbers. It was a widespread practice among the underage high school patrons to carefully remove the plastic numbers with a razor and glue them back on, to change one's date of birth to meet the legal drinking age.

It was at one of these weekend outings that I met Victor. He was searching for his date, my future college roommate, and asked me if I had seen her. Raised by my mother to be brutally honest, I responded that she was outside in a car with a former boyfriend. He ran outside to search for her. He found her kissing her former boyfriend in a parked car. Victor was so angry and his pride was so hurt that he hit the car's windows as they sat inside, with the doors securely locked and windows rolled up. He dared them to come out of the car. Finally, after releasing his anger on the car, he gave up and said that she was not worth the trouble.

The next weekend, at The Campus Club, Victor asked me if I'd like to go on a date with him. I wasn't certain if he and my friend's relationship was over, so I turned him down. A week later, he asked me to go to dinner. By then, it was obvious that my friend was dating her former boyfriend and had no interest in Victor. He seemed very nice, and his Italian good looks were hard to turn down: green eyes, dark wavy hair, stylish sideburns, and a strong chin with a dimple dead center. We went on our first date on March 14, my sister Karen's birthday.

Victor had dislocated his shoulder playing football, so he wore a sling on our first date. We ate dinner and danced most of the night, arm sling and all. The song that memorialized our first date was "You Are the Sunshine of My Life." It wasn't long after our first date that we were talking about marrying.

We had to keep our relationship a secret from my mother, though; I knew she would not approve of me dating anyone until I finished college. Not once had I ever introduced her to a date, so I wasn't going to start now. My dates had to meet me at a friend's house. As far as my mother knew, I had never dated. One suitor, not knowing how strict my mother was, came to my house bearing an Easter gift, a stuffed pink rabbit. I was horrified when I saw him walking up our driveway and opened the front door before he could ring the bell. I made up some story to get rid of him before my mother arrived home.

My mother constantly preached that I needed to concentrate on studying, not men. There would be plenty of time to get married. Without question, she believed that I would go to college immediately after I graduated from high school. Through her real estate wheeling and dealing, and other businesses, she could now more than afford to send me to college. She had scrimped, saved, and worked like a dog to make her dream come true. I didn't want to disappoint her; I had not stepped down from my job as her protector. But something more powerful than my mother's dream became important to me: my growing love for Victor.

Victor and I wanted to spend every moment together. If we couldn't be together, we talked on the phone several times a day. I also grew very close to his large family. He lived with his mother, two sisters, two brothers, and two dogs. His father had died of cancer when Victor was a teenager.

Victor's family was fun and lively. Although they had little money, their home was rich in love and laughter. They also fought like cats and dogs, something I had never experienced in my home, where we had to treat one another with the utmost politeness.

Victor's mother, Josephine, fed her family wholesome, tasty meals on a school cafeteria worker's income. The job suited her just fine as the work hours allowed her to keep her Italian eye on the coming and goings of her five children. With an iron hand but a loving heart, she raised her children as best she could. I thought she was terrific and became very fond of her.

I wasn't certain how to address Victor's mother. I was uncomfortable addressing her by her first name, and it seemed too formal to call her by her last name, Mrs. Gayle. Victor's mother fit the stereotype of an Italian mom. She was short, stocky, gray-haired, kind, and overly protective of her children. She also possessed another female Italian attribute, large breasts that look like torpedoes. So I affectionately nicknamed her Torps.

At Victor's home, it was the family atmosphere that I loved most. Torps went out of her way to make me feel welcome. While allowing my mother to think that I was studying at the library, three out of five evenings I was sitting at the Gayle family's dinner table. Not once did Torps make me feel like an outsider. Her heart was larger than life. I grew very close to her.

I felt that Torps loved me unconditionally, unlike my mother, who had high expectations of me. She didn't judge me. I would confide in Torps, who would laugh when I told her funny stories. She always supported my side of a situation, no matter how wrong I might have been. My mother, on the other hand, would tell me I was wrong if that's what she believed. It was black and white. She put strong biases, like love, aside. Right was right, and wrong was wrong. She was my reality check.

Once, I tested Torps by lighting up a cigarette in front of her. *Would she still care about me if she knew I smoked?* Torps continued to carry on a conversation with me without flinching. The next time I picked her up from work, she handed me a pack of cigarettes. That gesture proved that I could be as open with her as I wanted. It was comforting to know that I had someone I could talk to about anything and everything, without fear of disapproval.

Victor and I became engaged on November 22, 1973, five months after I graduated from high school. I didn't have the heart or courage to tell my mother about my engagement, so I asked Torps, who'd never met my mother, to talk to her. Torps knew that we'd run off and get married regardless of whether we received their consent, so she agreed.

Finally, the day arrived when Torps would meet my mother and deliver the news of our impending marriage. She and Victor sat in the living room with my mother and me. Mom was in shock when Torps told her that I was engaged to her son. After getting over the initial shock of not even knowing that I was dating Victor, she saw her vision of me attending college evaporate in front of her eyes. "Why did I workee so hard?" she asked. "My daughter, she no even appreciate."

Torps tried to reassure her that I would be very happy married to Victor. My mother turned to Victor and peppered him with questions. "How many houses do you own? You finish college? You own business?"

Victor just squirmed in the chair. Torps saw his discomfort and answered on his behalf. "He is too young to own property. My son is smart and a hard worker. Don't worry, Moon, Susan won't starve." But she saw that my mother wasn't too happy with the answers. She added, "I'm sure they'll save enough money to buy a house in the future."

That got my mother going again. "What? No house? No business? No nothing? Just get married?" She was shocked. As if Victor and I were not present, she said, "Why they marry? They own nothing. Whatza wrong with these people?"

Torps, in her gentle way, told Mom that she needed to support us or we'd run off and get married anyway. We were in love, and nothing would change that. They talked for a long time. In the end, Torps calmed my mother's fears.

My mother liked Torps. She thought she would be a good mother-in-law. In Korea, a wife's happiness was very dependent on her mother-in-law's goodwill toward her, especially if a woman married the eldest son, as in my case. A good-natured mother-in-law was no small matter with Korean parents, especially since my destiny, as my mother viewed it, would be to care for her.

My mother didn't waste any time planning my wedding. She depended on Torps to tell us the proper things to do. Being part of a large Italian family, Torps had attended as many weddings as funerals. Of course, the wedding had to be conducted by a Catholic priest. All good Italian weddings had little Italian wedding favors for the guests, so we chose the traditional favor, three white sugarcoated almonds, housed in a bag made of white net and tied with a white ribbon. The almonds were supposed to represent the couple and their children. Unbeknownst to us at the time, we literally fulfilled the tradition's meaning.

My mother handled the wedding preparations with the same intensity as she tackled any job. No big deal. No whining. She just did it, around the clock, until it was completed. I wasn't asked to choose a wedding dress, although I was useful as a mannequin. My mother decided that she would sew my wedding dress. She wasn't going to try to make me feel good by giving me any choices, when she didn't see any point to it. She'd do the best she could, and that would be that. She also thought she could sew a nicer-looking wedding dress than what we could find (and afford) in a store. I wish I'd known then what I came to appreciate much later; that dress would have meant so much more.

My mother sewed my wedding dress without a pattern. The dress was white satin with very simple lines. Hundreds of little buttons were covered with small pieces of satin material. They were hand sewn to the back and sleeves of the dress. My mother and her sister labored over the dress day and night. Finally, it was finished. I was so proud of my wedding dress. I pictured myself walking down the aisle in the dress and flowing veil. Until that moment, I hadn't been excited about the wedding ceremony.

Victor and I married on May 4, 1974. Over a hundred guests attended the ceremony. By the time I walked down the aisle, I was so nervous and excited that when we knelt at the church's altar in front of the priest, my knees shook so much that the kneeler rocked. I appreciated that I had someone, Frank, to give me away.

We went from the little chapel, located on the Fort Myer military base, to the officer reception hall in a black carriage pulled by white horses. I felt like Cinderella in her pumpkin.

The well-wishers greeted us warmly when we entered the reception hall. After eating and dancing, the photographer announced it was time for a family picture. He meant the immediate family: groom, bride, parents, grandparents, brother, and sister. In Korea, however, all of the aunts, uncles, and first, second, and third cousins, as well as close family friends, consider themselves immediate family. Fifteen Koreans converged on Victor and me to be part of the "immediate family" photograph. Victor looked a little startled as my Korean family jostled to be included in the family photo. Victor's siblings and mother managed to squeeze in to the small crowd so they could be included in the family photo.

Now I can appreciate how difficult it was for my mother to pay for my wedding reception. Although she was busily buying property, she was always cash poor. Her cash was tied up in the few houses she owned, and trying to help her large Korean family financially. She did the best she could; reluctantly using the money she had saved for my college fund toward our wedding. She figured I'd never attend college as a married woman. Family responsibilities would take precedence.

We easily transitioned to married life. Victor became a skilled plumber and I worked as a clerk typist for the Department of the Navy. Both jobs were near our new residence, a basement apartment in a home owned by Victor's grandmother. We were too young to realize how little we had. We thought we had it all.

As a young couple, we loved to entertain our friends. We'd have thirteen to fifteen friends over for dinner and drinks almost every weekend, early on in our marriage. I enjoyed the freedom after living under Mom's strict rules. I could stay up all night if I felt like it.

Since we lived next door to Victor's siblings, who were close to us in age but too young to leave home, they'd wander over whenever they felt like it. Victor's siblings lived in the house with their mother, grandmother, and uncle. We enjoyed their company, too.

My brother Eddie didn't visit us. We'd hear about him through my mother. Mainly, she would tell us how worried she was about him taking drugs. Karen, my little admirer, would come to our house on the weekends to hang out. She'd do anything I asked of her.

In addition to friends and family, we collected all kinds of animals: dogs, cats, fish, birds, and even a pig. My mother would complain when she visited our home, "What kind of people live with so much animal fur and bird feathers flying everywhere?" The pig in our hall closet was too much for her. She'd say, as she would many more times to come, "You people crazy."

***

Our happiness was short-lived. Six months after my marriage to Victor, tragedy struck. It happened suddenly and without warning.

The only thing unusual about the day was that I was shopping for Christmas gifts in November. Typically, I shop the week of Christmas. However, that year I was excited to shop early, so I could pick out some cute outfits for Karen, who would be turning thirteen in March. Victor's sister, Maryanne, accompanied me. Unlike me at age thirteen, I wanted Karen to return to school after the holidays in trendy clothes. Maryanne helped me select pants, shirts, and other clothing from a pre-teen department at a clothing store in the local mall.

When we finished shopping for the day, we were exhausted. We stopped by Maryanne's apartment to drop off the presents. I feared that Karen would find the gifts during one of her frequent visits if I hid them in my small living quarters.

Before she could put the key in the door's lock, the phone began ringing. We dropped our packages and Maryanne fumbled to unlock the door. She ran to the phone and picked up the receiver just in time. Out of breath, she answered, "Hello? What! Oh my God."

By the tone of her voice, I knew something bad had happened. I stopped dead in my tracks. Somehow, I knew I wouldn't like the news. Maryanne and I were close to many of the same people.

She continued to listen, pressing the phone against her face. Her face turned very pale and her eyes avoided mine.

I knew it had to be really bad news.

With the phone still to her ear, she finally turned and looked at me. "You'd better go to the hospital. Quick. Your sister. Your sister...she's been in a car accident. My mother thinks her leg is broken."

I said, "Call Victor; tell him to meet me at the hospital." Then I turned back. "Are you sure that's all? She just broke her leg?"

"That's what my mother told me. Karen is at Arlington Hospital."

As I drove to the hospital, thoughts raced through my head. I was so glad it was just a broken leg, but I couldn't help wondering all the while if it was worse, while at the same time pushing bad thoughts out of my mind.

But I couldn't stop the thoughts. *I wonder if it is worse; after all, I never shop this early for Christmas presents. Why did I think of her? Why was I buying her clothes? Is this a sign? No, she is okay.* I couldn't imagine life without her.

At twelve years old, Karen Marie was growing more beautiful every day. She was sweet, kind, and innocent. Her face seemed to dance in front of me, smiling, always smiling.

I remember how Eddie and I used to lovingly tease Karen. Her image becomes crystal clear. Silky black hair, parted on one side. Smooth skin which always looked tanned. Big, innocent, and toothy smile.

It was only a week ago that she'd helped me clean, cook, and do whatever I needed around the house. She seemed so happy to be part of my new married life. After all, I was her big sister. And she had a crush on Victor's two younger brothers, who were close to her in age and lived next door to us.

***

In the hospital bed lay my little sister. She looked to be napping peacefully. Her long black hair spread out on the pillow like those oriental fans we used to play with as children. Her black eyelashes gently brushed her cheeks.

I thought, *She looks pretty good, despite the tubes in her nose. I guess I panicked for nothing.* I turned toward a noise, air being pushed into her small frame. Her chest gently moving up and down with the rhythm of the pump. I thought, *The pump of life.*

Just as I breathed a sigh of relief, the doctor arrived and announced Karen's prognosis.

"Most likely she will not survive without a ventilator. If she does, she will be extremely brain damaged, most likely in a vegetative state."

Thoughts in my head spin—faster and faster. I silently held myself together. This was too much, too soon. *Damn it, I let myself hope for the best and look what I got.* The bottom of my world seemed to open up to a big black hole.

*Get yourself together.* Then I asked as calmly as possible, "Are you sure there is no hope?"

The doctor slowly shook his head. "No, there is no hope."

My mother and I wanted to be sure that Karen had no chance of surviving before we could agree to remove her from life support. We tried everything—praying, hoping, crying, screaming. Nothing seemed to help.

Out of desperation, my mother and I decided to see a psychic. We wanted answers, knowing that there wouldn't be any other way to satisfy our emptiness. How could we remove Karen's life support without trying everything?

We met with a woman who came highly recommended by a close friend. We explained that my sister was in the hospital and we had to make some decisions regarding keeping her on life support.

The psychic looked at us sadly and said, "Something is missing between her head and neck area. She is already dead. Let her go. It's peaceful where she is going."

I said desperately, "Can't you see anything else?"

She simply responded, "No."

I broke down in tears. She had only confirmed what I knew in my heart had to be done. Let Karen go, in peace, with dignity.

My defenses were fully engaged, my mind racing. What were the next steps? The announcement to the rest of the family, my sister's friends, her school—and then her funeral. It was my way of dealing with something so mind-boggling that every bone hurt. You could feel it in your gut, that empty, hollow feeling.

Meanwhile, Mom sat in a cold vinyl hospital chair, looking dumbfounded and overcome with grief. Empty, hollow. Finally realizing that she wouldn't see her sweet child again, she cried out in anguish, "My beautiful daughter. Why her? I don't want to bury my daughter. I should have died first."

How many parents of children who have died prematurely have said the same thing?

I'd thought of calling our father to let him know, but we hadn't heard from him in years, so I decided not to. However, my mother called him in California. "Ed, your daughter is going to die. We won't take the breathing machine off of her until you come."

He said, "Do what you have to do; I won't be coming."

Mom couldn't believe what she was hearing. Sweet Karen's own father didn't want a last chance to kiss her warm cheek? Unbelievable. Another heart-stopping blow. My mother sobbed and sobbed, repeating, "How could someone be so coldhearted?"

But despite all of the hurt and pain my father caused by his uncaring decision, my mother never moved from her position of being grateful to him for bringing us to the United States.

From what we could piece together about Karen's accident, she had returned to school to retrieve her hat, which someone had teasingly taken. She had taken her new bike with her. As a trained safety guard, she knew that she had to walk her bike across the busy eight-lane highway that children crossed to walk to Thomas Jefferson Middle School. She crossed lanes one, two, three, four, five, six, seven, and boom. The light changed. She'd almost made it across all the lanes of traffic.

But the green light meant that cars already traveling at speeds of fifty-five miles per hour or greater could continue to roar down the highway. A car in the far right eastbound lane hit Karen. The driver accelerated, seemingly trying to leave the scene, but Karen and her bike were entangled under his car, which forced him to stop.

Onlookers grabbed the driver before he could flee. They were horrified to see the little girl tangled up in her bicycle under the car. She appeared lifeless, but she was breathing.

This tragedy shouldn't have happened. That seemed to be the common outcry expressed by the media, friends, and family. Parents in the local area were outraged at the senseless death, something they felt could have been avoided. They pressured the county to make the highway safer for pedestrians, especially the students.

A reporter for the local newspaper, *The Arlington County Journal*, reported that although two additional traffic lanes had been opened recently, the county had failed to increase the timing on the traffic light. The newspapers reported that Karen only had twelve seconds to cross all eight lanes of traffic.

Cars frequently sped upward of seventy miles per hour in a fifty-five-mile-per-hour zone. The county denied any wrongdoing, stating that there had been only two deaths in the past five years. They failed to note that Karen's death occurred on the second day after the two new lanes opened on Route 50. The timing on the traffic lights did not allow enough time for pedestrians to cross the busy highway.

A newspaper reporter tested the county's contention that pedestrians had plenty of time to cross the broadened highway. The six-foot-tall *Arlington Journal* news reporter stood at the curb of the highway. As soon as the light changed, he began walking swiftly across the highway. He barely made it across the highway before the light changed to green.

So, in response to the community's request, the county built a pedestrian overpass over Route 50, the highway where the car struck my sister.

The local newspapers ran her story. Karen's smiling face innocently looked out at readers. About 60 schoolmates attended her funeral. She was buried in the pink handmade gown she wore as a bridesman in my wedding. The newspaper also featured a picture of my mother, grief stricken, head lowered, hands clasped in front of her, slowly leaving her young daughter's grave. She was being assisted by Frank, unable to walk unaided. Although the newspaper pictures were in black and white, they were vivid. Another memory to add to life's album—one that I wish I could tear up, and start over with a different outcome.

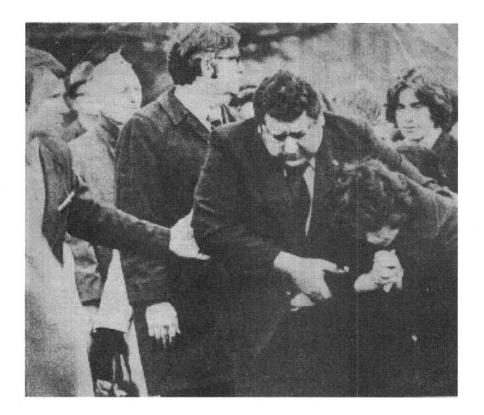

Frank supporting Moon Ja

Those closest to Karen dealt with her death differently. I relied on my belief that there must be a purpose for this tragedy, beyond what I could see. I could only go on in life by believing that God knew best. He knows the contents of the entire film of life, while I could see only one frame.

Eddie dealt with the pain by avoiding it. He grew more reclusive and secretive. Almost on the first anniversary of our sister's death, Eddie, at age sixteen, was charged with burglary and sent to Beaumont Learning Center, a juvenile detention facility.

Frank blamed himself for Karen's death. Since Karen was only five years old when Frank came into our lives, he considered her his daughter. They were very close. He bought the bike that Karen was walking across the highway when she was killed. He also believed that had he been home at his normal time, Karen never would have returned to the school. Although Frank didn't show his emotions, it was obvious that his suffering was very deep. It seemed like overnight he became a weakened old man, at the age of forty-four.

Mom did what she typically did when faced with tragedy. She worked like a dog. If she had free time, the pain would be unbearable. Work made her forget. One thing that indicated the depth of her pain was that she literally rid herself of anything musical in her life. My mother loved listening to Nat King Cole or Tony Bennett. She also enjoyed the strong emotions evoked by soul and country music. Music struck a chord in her. But now, she didn't want her emotions stirred. She gave away her hi-fi stereo and record albums. Perhaps she didn't think she deserved to be happy after Karen's death. I'll never know for sure.

***

Death did something to me. Ironically, it made me appreciate life. After my sister's premature death, I wanted to do something more with my life. I tried to make my government clerical job as interesting as possible, taking on more and more responsibility, to the point that I was doing the work of senior-level professionals. It wasn't enough. I was bored and restless. The only thing separating me from the "professionals" was a college degree.

As I considered applying for college, I could hear my mom saying, "Sujan, no one can take your education away from you. Even if you lost everything you own, you will always have your education."

I also spoke to a friend at work about my desire to return to college. We agreed that we didn't want to be typing for a bunch of idiots at the age of forty. We decided to enroll in the local community college to test the waters. I wasn't confident I could get back into the swing of things, after being out of school for three years. I also couldn't stop working full time; my paycheck was a necessity.

After completing a few semesters, my colleague from work stopped going to college. I continued to attend, although it was very difficult juggling marriage, my mother's businesses, work, and school. I also believed that I had to study five times harder than the other students. I'd hear students talking about partying all night, then I'd see them ace a difficult exam—compared to me, who had stayed up half the night studying to barely earn a B.

But I didn't give up. I just studied harder. In the subjects where I was weakest, I would befriend the smartest student in the class. We'd meet and study together. We'd also challenge one another on the topic. Learning was easier when I actively participated. I also learned how to study and memorize large volumes of facts and timelines through self-help study literature.

I mapped it all out. By attending classes part-time, I would be finished with my bachelor's degree in eight years. It seemed daunting for a twenty-one-year-old. To keep myself motivated, I'd tell myself, *Whether I attend college or not, eight years from now, I'll be twenty-nine years old. So why not attend college, earn a degree, and have an interesting career?*

# CHAPTER 14

In January 1977, my mother, at age forty-five, bought The Country Hut, a small restaurant/bar in Alexandria, Virginia, near Crystal City. Patrons, mainly railroad workers from across the street, referred to it as The Hut.

Five months later, my son Jason was born. When I was admitted to the hospital to deliver him, my mother and Frank couldn't come to the hospital until after midnight because they didn't have anyone to cover for them at The Hut. When they arrived, Victor's family packed the waiting room. Frank became so worried about me being in labor for more than twenty hours that he threatened the doctors. "You better be taking good care of Susan or I'll do a Mexican tap dance on your heads."

Following Jason's birth, my mother would try to squeeze in time to visit her first grandchild. His birth made her realize that she was getting older. Even though he was too young to understand, Mom would say to him, "I don't want you to call me grandma. You call me Mama Moon. Then I stay young."

It wasn't long after Jason was born that Mom became ill. Her leg began to swell and discolor from pulling twenty-hour shifts. Her doctor explained that her earlier radiation treatment for cancer caused her leg to swell, resulting in a serious infection because of overuse. A couple of months later, Frank was hospitalized. He may have had a second heart attack.

With no one to manage and operate The Hut, Victor resigned from his job to take on the onerous task. He worked one hundred forty hours a week trying to keep the place going. He cooked, cleaned, interviewed bands, ordered food, paid vendors, and reconciled the cash register.

A country band would entertain customers on the weekends. It turned out to be a hangout for rowdy blue-collar workers. Fights would break out frequently. Drunken customers used glass bottles or cups as weapons. Plastic soon replaced glass.

When Victor wasn't breaking up fights, he feared being robbed. The place had been broken into several times. One time, the robbers entered the building by cutting through the roof. A particularly scary incident involved a customer in a long black trench coat entering the restaurant. He looked around as if scoping out the place.

Victor was alone, standing behind the counter. He asked the customer, "How can I help you?" The man casually walked to the counter, his hand was in his coat pocket. He pushed out his coat pocket as if he had a gun in it and demanded the money from the cash register. Victor thought that he looked like the suspect at large who had murdered employees at a Roy Rogers restaurant. It was a vicious murder of young kids. The man had locked their dead bodies in the restaurant's walk-in refrigerator.

Victor reached under the counter to retrieve a bag to hand over the money. At that moment, he thought, *This guy is going to think I'm pulling a gun. I'm dead.* Suddenly, the door opened. Both Victor and the would-be robber turned to the incoming customers, who walked toward the counter, shouting, "How are you doing, Vic?" The would-be robber turned to Vic and said in a low voice, "I'm just kidding." He then turned and quickly left.

After a few months, Mom and Frank felt well enough to work at The Hut. However, they could no longer work the hours necessary to maintain the business. Victor stayed on to help. In addition, Victor's mother began working at The Hut. I was dumbfounded. Torps, the devout Catholic who never left her home, tending bar?

My mother convinced her to work at The Hut. She told her that she needed to get out of the house. "You've done enough for your five children. You have good personality to work with people. Please help me."

Torps loved it! She started dying her hair and fixing herself up. She could be heard humming and was in good spirits, whereas before she always looked tired and worn out. The railroad guys flirted with her. She'd call them "little bastards" (a term of endearment). She didn't need to worry about being harmed. The railroad guys would have laid their lives on the line if anyone had tried to hurt her.

She also found love, something she never thought she'd find in a bar, and eventually remarried. My mother took full credit for that happy event. "Mrs. Gayle needed to meet men. She was good mother—always make her children happy. Now she deserve to be happy too."

\*\*\*

In December 1978, approximately a year and half after Jason was born, my mother, after searching for years, finally reunited with her Korean-born son, Woon Gee. My mother's family thought she was asking for trouble, reopening an old wound.

When Woon Gee had contacted my mother's family in the past, he'd been discouraged from finding her. He was told she had died, or that she was in the United States, married to an American. In other words, "Stop looking for her." Woon Gee's earlier feelings of abandonment and rejection deepened.

When she found him, Mom began the long application process of bringing Woon Gee and his family to the United States. First, she had to prove she was his biological mother. The Korean census record listed Mr. Yeo's second wife as Woon Gee's mother. My mother had to find people who would sign affidavits that she was his birth mother.

I'm not certain how many years passed, but shortly after Woon Gee's U.S. immigration paperwork was executed, he, his wife, and their young daughter and baby boy arrived to the United States. Woon Gee was twenty-nine, a few years older than his wife.

My mother and I were anxious on the day he was due to arrive. We didn't know what to expect. Would he be bitter? Would he fit in with the rest of the family? What did he look like? Would we like his wife? Would he like us? After all these years of hearing stories about our older brother who had been left behind, we wanted to welcome him to our family. We also wanted to see our mother happy.

Finally, my mother's eldest son would be near her. I was hopeful that she could finally rid herself of feeling guilty for leaving Woon Gee with his father. The first son played an important role in the Korean culture. He and his wife were responsible for taking care of the son's mother—my mother. But, at age forty-six, my mother had many more years before she'd need help of that kind.

Besides, she didn't want to depend on her son—or anyone, for that matter. Since separating from my father, the only person that she fully trusted was herself. She had hoped that her eldest son would take care of her businesses, but giving up her authority or sharing her bank accounts with others was another story. Mom had a way of moving between two very different cultures. Whichever suited her own interests at the time was the one she adopted for the situation.

Whatever hopes she had of living happily ever after with her Korean son and his family were dashed after an incident that brought back all her memories of her nightmarish life with Mr. Yeo. Not too long after Woon Gee arrived, I spent the night at my mother's house. I awoke to hear people shouting in Korean from the living room downstairs.

I crept slowly down the stairs. I could hear my mother and Woon Gee shouting, although I couldn't tell whether they were arguing. Then I heard Woon Gee's wife crying softly.

My half brother looked up and seemed startled to see me standing there. Even a little ashamed. My mother looked extremely upset. As soon as my mother saw me, she cried out in anguish, "Woon Gee beat his wife! He just like his father. I should have listen to my sisters; they said I ask for trouble by bringing him to the United States."

I felt so bad for my mother, for Woon Gee's wife, and for the children. But I also agreed with my mother's family. *Why do you ask for trouble?*

From that point forward, my mother couldn't show Woon Gee affection, which made his insecurities worse. He would ask her to put lotion on his back, but she refused. She couldn't stomach being around him. She saw her ex-husband in him. "The apple doesn't fall far from the tree" certainly seemed to be the case.

Although Woon Gee's behavior toward his wife literally made my mother sick, she felt obligated to try to help her son achieve financial independence. But it was more out of obligation and guilt than love. Since she'd lost respect for Woon Gee, she didn't ask his opinion about business matters or include him in managing her properties.

About a month after Woon Gee's arrival, my mother bought a fifth property, at age forty-seven. It was located five minutes from our home in Arlington.

I just saw more work. I don't mean general cleaning; I mean hard labor. I did get somewhat of a reprieve on this property, however. My mother asked Woon Gee and his wife to help with cleaning and renovating her latest purchase. She quickly got them up to speed on tearing down walls, framing walls, hanging drywall, spackling, and painting.

Any thoughts Woon Gee might have had of his American mother living in the lap of luxury changed. She worked harder than most men, lifting, pulling, hammering, and drilling. She did it all. No job was too dirty or too difficult. "Just do it," she would say.

Soon, my mother discovered that Woon Gee was mechanically inclined. He seemed very bright and could fix just about anything; although without a college education, his career options were limited to working with his hands. My mother would get into spats with him on how to make repairs on her properties. We called it the "Moon-way" or the highway.

Finally, with the hope that he'd find a job, my mother introduced Woon Gee to a few Korean businessmen who owned gas stations and car repair shops. Eventually, he landed a job as a car mechanic. Mom purchased his first set of car mechanic tools. She wanted Woon Gee to buy his own gas station in the future. Of course, she recognized that she would have to help him financially.

***

Eventually, Woon Gee gave up on believing he'd be close to his mother, running her businesses, or caring for her when she grew old. His dreams of what life would be like when he reunited with his mother would never be a reality. Perhaps he would have been happier if he could have held on to his dreams of embracing his long lost "well-to-do" American mother. A mother who would make all of his insecurities go away. A mother who would make him feel whole by loving him unconditionally, pure and simple.

Unfortunately, Woon Gee couldn't overcome his insecurities. He wanted the two most important people in his life, his wife and his mother, to respect and love him. Ironically, these were the same people he'd hurt the most. His neediness manifested itself as being controlling and demanding, but he also had a side to him that was generous and loving.

Woon Gee demanded respect from his wife, rather than earning it. He told her to prepare a four-course dinner for him at least three times a day. He wanted her full attention. He worked near his house, so he could easily drive home to check on his wife and eat. Every day, his wife would prepare fresh rice, fish, soup, and three to five different Korean vegetables. Woon Gee seemed to use food to fill his emptiness. And despite his hearty appetite, he remained small in stature. My mother would say that he had a tapeworm.

Mom also confided in me how bad she felt when Woon Gee accused her of loving her American children more than him. She said that she couldn't deny her feelings. When she told him that he acted and looked like his father, there was nothing he could say. Those were the facts. And he didn't feel he could change those facts.

Woon Gee really did try to be a good son, a son that a mother would be proud of. But as much as Mom wanted to feel a bond with her Korean-born son, she just couldn't after she witnessed him abusing his wife. Woon Gee represented a ghost of her past—a most unwelcome guest. But at the same time, he was her eldest son.

## CHAPTER 15

Frank hadn't been back at The Hut long before he suffered a stroke, which left him speechless and paralyzed on his left side. He was hospitalized at Walter Reed Hospital in Washington, DC. It was sad to see him, a once healthy, proud, and strong man, lying in his own filth and unable to speak.

He had somehow managed to roll over on his left arm and hand. Since he was paralyzed, he had been unable to reposition his arm. From the large red indentation on his back, made by his balled-up fist, it appeared that he had been lying in that uncomfortable position for some time. His eyes followed us in the hospital room. He tried to speak but could only dribble spit.

My mother held his hand lovingly. She said, "You've been a good man. Thank you for helping me." I could see the love in his eyes as he looked back at her.

When Frank was able to leave the hospital, Mom took care of him. She would give him physical therapy by lifting his heavy legs repeatedly. Mainly, he stayed in a hospital bed my mother set up on the first floor. She would feed him and clean his bedpan. He never regained his speech. Frank died at home on July 7, 1979, at age forty-nine.

Death was starting to take a toll on my mother. As she had done in the past, she replaced sadness with work. The year following Frank's death, she bought another house, which occupied all of her time. So much so that, a month later, Mom leased the building where she operated The Hut and sold the business to the new tenants.

Mom recognized that Victor worked for practically nothing. However, all along she had a plan. When she sold the restaurant/bar business, she handed Victor a check for ten thousand dollars, a down payment for a house. She believed we'd never save enough for a down payment since we didn't manage our funds as she did—frugally.

***

Within a few months, my mother rented the new house to a tenant on government housing assistance. My mother thought it was wonderful that the government would help those in need. Mom assumed the tenant appreciated receiving rental assistance. However, my mother soon discovered—to her great dismay—that the tenant was far from being appreciative.

The tenant called the county for the most ridiculous reasons. She'd report that her "electric" didn't work. The county would stop rental payments to my mother until she fixed the problem. Mom always attempted to take care of repairs herself to save money. "If you have two strong hands, try to do it yourself," she would say, as she searched for a hammer or a screwdriver.

She knocked on the tenant's door. No answer. Knock, knock. Louder. Knock, knock. Finally, someone opened the door. At noon, the tenant was rubbing her eyes as if she'd just woken up. Apparently, she had. She said angrily, "Go away and come back at a decent hour!"

My mother shoved the door open and told her, "Get out my way. I'm a busy lady. I fixee your electric problem." It turned out to be an easy repair: unscrew the burnt-out light bulb and replace it with a new one. While changing the bulb, my mother lectured the woman about sleeping late, not working, and setting a bad example for her children.

Mom certainly wasn't bashful about telling other people how they should live their lives. I honestly think it was because she cared. She wanted people to know that they were capable of doing better if they were willing to work hard.

She thought the tenants receiving government assistance, although less financially well off than she, were actually "richer" because at least they had some basic American schooling. She assumed they could read and write English, since public school was free. Who wouldn't take advantage of a free education? My mother had a third-grade Korean education, and thought that if you knew only the fundamentals of reading and writing English, you could do and be anything you wanted.

She told me about another incident at the rental home, which made me fear for her life. Mom packed up her carpentry tools and cleaning supplies to repair yet another complaint the tenant made to the county. The stove wasn't working.

When she arrived at the property, it was the same old thing. She had to bang on the door and holler at the top of her lungs for someone to open the door.

"Uh, uh, uh," my mother muttered when she saw the grease and filth covering the stove. She knew that the flame on the grime-caked gas burners couldn't possibly light without oxygen. She started taking apart the stove burners in order to scrub each burner element.

While she was scrubbing the stove, a few of the residents in the house began waking up. They gathered in the kitchen. The children set out their cereal and milk on the kitchen table, but some of the adults evidently needed a little more of a kick to get them started. They retrieved a bottle of whiskey and set it on the small table. As the whiskey bottle emptied, the voices in the kitchen became louder. The extended family members were having a lively discussion, cursing, laughing, and just having a good old time.

Mom relayed, "They say tings like mudder pucker. Right in front of their children! So I can't stand it anymore. I say to them, how can you people just sit here drinking and cussing in front of your small children? You should get up early and work instead of waiting for the mailman to bring you a welfare check."

The "lady of the house," who was quite large, stood up and slowly walked toward Mom in an intimidating manner. When my mother didn't flinch, the woman stared at my mother in a threatening way. Then, she pointed her index finger about one inch from my mother's nose and put her other hand on her hip. Her eyes narrowed. "You better not be talking about me and my family. I'll kick your Chinese ass. And what do you mean by 'you people'? You got something against black folk?"

Although my mother was outnumbered five against one, she stood her ground. "I'm not talkee about black or white. I talkee about *you* and how bad *you* look in front of your children. Filthy mouth, drinking in front of your children. You, their mother. Why can't you teachee them the right way to live?"

I told Mom she needed to mind her own business so as not to endanger herself. She replied, "Sujan, you worry too much. Just because they poor people doesn't mean they want to hurt me. They just talk bad. They not raised right. They only know about welfare. Anyway, I'm not afraid to die. Everybody die. While you are alive, you can't act like a dead person. If you believe something, you have to speak. You have to speakee the truth."

## CHAPTER 16

The following year, in October 1981, at the age of forty-nine, Mom found a new property to buy. It was a rundown commercial building in Washington, DC, zoned for retail business on the ground floor. Three or four apartments were located on the second floor.

Prostitutes and drug dealers conducted their business right in front of the building. I pleaded with Mom not to buy it, worried sick about her working there. She only replied, "You worry too much. That's why you don't have money. You live paycheck to paycheck. You have to takee risk."

My mother went ahead and bought the building on the corner of V Street and 14th Street NW. She was so proud of her purchase that she wanted me to see it firsthand. I refused to go to the building, however. My mother looked hurt. I felt torn, but I was frightened to go to that area.

I just couldn't continue to allow her to control me with her pained looks. I had to take a stand. I didn't want to be in a place where pimps, drug dealers, and addicts hung out. And if I agreed to go to the building, Victor would be angry with me.

Even so, although I didn't want to be involved with the District of Columbia government, I ended up having to help my mother complete forms and navigate through the Landlord and Tenant Court. That whole experience was a low point in my life. I wouldn't do it again for a million bucks.

The ground floor of the building was unoccupied. "We cannot waste space; I havee to rent right away," Mom said. First, she had to find a new crew of local "laborers." Alongside her crew, she cleaned up the filth, debris, and mess left by the homeless people who had taken up residence in the empty space: urine, defecation, rotting food, vomit, rodents. The worst of the worst was contained in that little building that my mother cherished with all her heart.

Since she couldn't read, she relied on hearsay. Before she'd buy a property, she attempted to find out the scoop on the area. She'd visit local coffee shops or just talk to the locals. Rumor was that a municipal building was going to be built across the street, and the Green Line Metro subway would be up the street in the near future.

Armed with this information, she decided that the area could use a carryout restaurant. People who work in office buildings, especially big ones like the municipal government building, would need a place nearby to grab a sandwich. Mom thought the ideal carryout location would be in the vacant corner space of her new building. She also wanted to sell beer. Obtaining a new beer and wine license in Washington, DC, however, was no easy feat.

Of course, Mom had no idea how to navigate the District of Columbia building and zoning regulatory departments—but she knew how to find the courthouse. From there, she kept asking different people where the zoning office was located until she was successful. Then, she tried to find a helpful person to assist her in completing the paperwork, or tell her what was needed.

Government workers were willing to tell her what she needed to do, although some of them lost patience with her poor English. She didn't get much help on completing forms, so she'd bring her paperwork to my house and anxiously wait for me to arrive home from work.

That was the last thing I wanted to do after working all day, and before eating dinner. But we'd sit down at my kitchen table to review and complete the forms. Mom didn't know half the answers to the questions, or even where to find the answers. Therefore, one simple form could take hours—or even days—to complete. Unfortunately, there were many, many forms to complete. Here's a typical exchange:

"Mom, what is the building's lot number?"

"How am I supposed to know?"

"You must have settlement papers or something with the lot and square number, right?"

"If I knew that, then I wouldn't be asking you to fill out my forms."

"Mom, I'm getting really tired, and I can't complete this form for you if you aren't more helpful."

"Ah, you don't want to do anything for me."

"Mom, you really need to hire an attorney. You need to evict people, you need to change the zoning, you need to apply for building permits, you need to apply for a food establishment license..." The list would go on.

As usual, my mother thought an attorney was a waste of money, especially since I could read and write English. I couldn't seem to make her understand that I really didn't have the legal experience or education to be helpful in this endeavor. She wouldn't hear of it.

"You do it for me. I need your help."

I felt like yelling, "How much more do I have to do for you before you'll just stop? I have my own life!" Those words were not spoken aloud, though. I didn't want to hurt my mother's feelings. She'd been through too much pain and hurt.

Mom and I would go frequently to the courthouse to turn in paperwork and complete additional paperwork. We attended long hearings to listen to people debate about whether my mother should be allowed to open the carryout place. I was so tired of it all, but she continued to fight even after I pleaded for her to just give up.

The application also required community support. If my mother could round up enough supporters who were willing to sign a petition supporting a carryout location that served food and beer, then she might have a chance of receiving approval.

But next to her DC building was a Catholic church, which also ran a day-care center. Why would she think a church might want to support a carryout restaurant that served beer? Also, the area was predominantly black, and the conflicts between the African American community and small Korean business owners had been steadily escalating over the years. Why would she think the community would have any desire to support her?

I had great doubts that my mother could get even one person to sign her petition. She would have liked me to help her collect signatures, but there was no way I was going to walk up and down those streets. I read too much news about women getting mugged, raped, or killed in the District of Columbia. I feared for my mother's safety. But she wouldn't listen to me.

My mother had a little politician in her. She walked the streets with her petition and asked people to sign it, explaining that she wanted to fix up the building to make the neighborhood pretty, and to open a nice carryout place, where people could get good food. I think she was able to sell her idea to the church, at least, because without their support I doubt she could have gone any further. The church probably viewed a new carryout location as the lesser of two evils: Homeless people living next door and defecating on the floors, or a carryout restaurant? We'll choose the carryout place.

On the other hand, my mother wasn't shy when it came to business. She walked right up to prostitutes, pimps, dealers, and drug addicts and asked them to sign. They lived in the neighborhood, so why wouldn't they count? All of them signed her petition.

Months later, she was successful. My mother could open her carryout location, and her beer and wine license was approved. I hadn't seen her so happy in a long time. She beamed with pride. "See, I tell you this not so hard. You have to keep trying."

I wasn't off the hook yet. Now I had to complete all of the applications to obtain building permits. Everything had to be installed: plumbing, electric, carpentry, the whole nine yards. I was in the courthouse so frequently that staff started asking me if I was an attorney. Would this ever end? Not as far as my mother was concerned.

The biggest headache was evicting the current tenants. It took about a year. One by one, we would go through the drill of sending eviction notices and wait for our turn at the landlord-tenant court. The tenants didn't show up for court because they knew they didn't have to. Finally, the court issued judgments that officially gave my mother the right to evict tenants who had not paid rent in years. But the tenants knew the eviction game better than we did. I think it's called "playing the system."

I called the marshal's office to evict the tenants. Busy tone. I dialed again. Busy tone. This went on for an hour. Finally, the phone rang. A recording stated that the time to schedule a marshal was over and to try back the next day. Talk about frustrating. This went on for months. Finally, I reached someone in the marshal's office. They explained that they were backlogged. There were thousands of evictions ahead of ours.

My mother had a mortgage payment; she couldn't wait a year or more for a marshal to evict the tenants. And get this: the tenants still had the right to complain if living conditions didn't meet their standards!

Mom took matters into her own hands. She scaled up a ladder, crawled across the window overhang, and climbed through the window to gain access to the apartment! The tenants were shocked to see their Korean landlady entering their apartment through a window in broad daylight. They exclaimed, "Lady, you've got a lot of guts! I'm going to stab you in the stomach with this knife if you don't get the hell out of here!"

My mother stood her ground. She said, "I don't move. I work too hard for you to sit up here drinking and taking drugs. You don't pay me rent. You leave." After hours of shouting back and forth, and days of my mother stalking the tenants, they eventually gave up and left. They told her she was crazy, and that if she wasn't careful, she'd end up dead. After all, this was not her neighborhood.

With the tenants out of her building, Mom started hiring people off the streets. They stole her tools every opportunity they could. But as long as they worked for her, she took care of them. She worked side by side with them, demanding that they work harder: "Get up. You, young man, help me carry this."

And this would go on for hours, days, and weeks.

She opened her carryout place in record time. Of course, she wasn't going to let just anyone handle the cash; she stayed behind the cash register. At night, she would clean the grease from the grills and the floor. Then, she would sleep on a mattress on the floor to guard her business from all of the thieves that roamed the streets at night. I gave up worrying about her. She was going to do what she wanted to do. No one—I mean no one—could tell her what to do.

One day she was a powerhouse of energy. She could work around the clock, nonstop, to the point where she couldn't move her fingers. She would use a pencil to push the cash register buttons. But then one moment, just a split second in her life, and things were completely different.

She was walking on the greasy floor when she slipped and fell. Her leg, damaged earlier from the radiation treatments for her cancer and working long hours at The Hut, swelled to the point of turning black. Reddish and purplish steaks ran up and down her leg, and she was forced to be hospitalized again. But this time it was worse; the doctors said that they might have to amputate her leg.

From that day on, she felt like she lost her power. The doctors said that her lymph nodes were destroyed from the radiation treatments. The fall had exacerbated this condition. Her leg remained swollen for the rest of her life. If she stood too long, it would swell, turn different colors, and ache like a toothache. She could no longer run away from her problems, and consequently, she became increasingly depressed.

Eventually, she sold the DC carryout business for the amount she'd paid for the entire building. She leased the other part of the building to a drug rehabilitation center, which was always behind in paying rent. But Mom had a soft spot for drug rehabilitation centers, since Eddie was a drug abuser.

## CHAPTER 17

Mom's and my dream for me to complete college was finally realized when I graduated from George Washington University with a bachelor's degree in psychology. Years earlier, I had transferred my credits from a community college.

Although a career as a psychologist no longer interested me, I was fulfilled to have earned a college degree while being responsible for holding down a full-time job, caring for Jason, performing bookkeeping duties for Mom's and Victor's separate businesses, and keeping up as best I could with housekeeping.

I had wanted to use my education to help abused children, but my two-year stint working as an intern in a battered women's shelter convinced me that I wouldn't be content in a psychologist's role. It seemed like all I did in the shelter was to keep it alive by filling out one form after another. There was too much red tape involved in a nonprofit. Then I found that I couldn't help the children. If I managed to get them out of their current situation, where would they go? They didn't want to leave their parents.

I noted with disdain that the counselors, with their MSW and PhD degrees, didn't seem satisfied with their career choice. Somewhere along the way, they had lost their genuine desire to help others. They complained about their minimum-wage jobs. Well, if I was going to end up hating my profession, then I might as well make some money. My idealism died in that shelter.

If not psychology, then what? I liked working with people and solving problems, improving things. So I entered George Washington's master's program and majored in human resource management. I could work with people, make a decent salary, help develop company leaders, and make the business operations and administration more efficient. I knew I couldn't continue at my former pace—working full time, attending graduate school, and raising Jason. If I quit my job, I couldn't afford to pay for a master's degree.

Victor and I concluded that the only way we could afford for me to attend graduate school full time would be to rent our house and move to my mother's house. We both knew that Mom wasn't the easiest person to live with. We also recognized that we'd be in middle of her constant storm. She didn't seem happy without some type of chaos swirling around. If the storm died down, she might have to face her demons.

I knew what my mother would say. She would never turn me down, or any other relative who asked for help. When I spoke to my mother about my desire to earn my master's degree, she practically cried with joy. She was in disbelief when I graduated with my bachelor's degree. Now I was ready to earn a master's degree. She never thought it possible for a married woman to get a college degree. She was especially proud that my motivation and drive to earn my degree never wavered after Jason was born. "Of course you and your family can move in with me. I help you as much as I can." Indeed, she did. She allowed us to stay rent free and paid for most of my master's program.

***

My mother was more active than most people were, but she had to work at a slower pace, because of her swollen leg. She loved good deals, which usually meant the item was free or at below market price. Even if she didn't need it, she might just have a use for it later.

Like the time she asked us to move restaurant equipment out of a restaurant that was closing. She said, "Everything is free. Restaurant equipment is expensive. I might need it later." I thought, *Now how is she going to open a restaurant with her bad leg?* But we knew we couldn't reason with her—and we were living at her home for nothing. So off we went.

Little did we know that she would want us to remove all of the ceiling tiles and light fixtures. The stainless steel restaurant equipment was heavy. Deep fryers, grills, even plumbing fixtures—you name it, we hauled it away. We worked for at least ten hours, finally stopping at three or four in the morning. Alongside us was my mother, bad leg and all.

Then there was the time a motel was remodeling and giving away its furnishings. Mom wanted us to remove all of the drapes, tables, chairs, dressers, and bed frames from about fifty rooms. I had no idea what she was going to do with all this stuff, but she managed to use most of it. The rest was stored for a rainy day.

Eddie wasn't living at Mom's home, so he must have been incarcerated. I recalled my mother saying that he was in a federal prison. Mom had wanted me to visit him; I refused. She was upset that I wasn't being helpful and loving toward my brother.

Mom didn't like being alone in her house. Thus, before we had moved in with her, she had rented a room to a religious fanatic, Mr. Sorrel. My mother thought he was a wonderful person because he was deeply religious. He carried his Bible with him all the time, so he could convert sinners. He'd preach on subways, street corners, anywhere he could capture someone's attention.

We moved into the bedroom across the hall from Mr. Sorrel. He was impeccable in his dress, looking like he'd walked out of the forties era. He wore a bow tie, a white starched dress shirt, and a black suit. It was his uniform. He had thinning, light-colored hair, and he was tall, pale, and thin. He scrubbed his face so hard it shone. I guess he took the adage cleanliness is next to godliness to heart.

The tenant was yet another eccentric person among a growing collection. My mother seemed to attract them like fireflies. Every morning, Mr. Sorrel went through his ritual. First, he'd eat out of a can; we could hear his spoon scraping the inside of the can to get the last bit of food. Then, he would sing the National Anthem while he bathed. He couldn't carry a tune. When he was planning a trip out of town, he'd call every morning to confirm his reservation, up to the date of his departure. Good God, he wasn't leaving for his trip for another three months.

Mom also invited the strangest people to her home and fed them. I recall a mentally ill couple that my mother invited. They rented a bungalow from Mom, situated in the backyard in her first Arlington home. Their names were Josie and Mike. Josie appeared to be in her forties; Mike in his twenties. Josie looked more like Mike's mother than a girlfriend. I heard that they'd met in a substance abuse halfway house. They made an odd pair, to say the least, but they seemed to be in love.

My mother felt sorry for Josie and tried to befriend her. She said that Josie had had a hard life and was abused both in her childhood and in adulthood. When Josie would come over for coffee or a meal, she'd make herself right at home. Mom tried to make Josie a cup of hot coffee and carry on a conversation with her. But Josie preferred cold coffee. We used instant coffee, however, which would only dissolve in hot water.

Josie would use cold water, instead of stirring the instant coffee into hot water and allowing the coffee to cool. She'd sip the coffee as if it were hot; all the while, the un-dissolved instant coffee grounds would form a moustache on her upper lip. She seemed oblivious to the accumulation. She just kept rambling and sipping her coffee.

Half her teeth were missing. The other half were rotten. She had red lipstick smeared all over her mouth. And she was wearing a bra on the outside of her shirt. When she squatted on the kitchen chair, in spread-eagle fashion, I could see that she wasn't wearing underwear!

I whispered to my mother that Josie was disgusting. Mom just laughed and said, "She can't help it if she crazee. She a nice woman. She just have a hard life. You can see that she used to be a pretty lady." Josie didn't seem capable of doing much, other than drinking cold coffee and chain-smoking.

Mike's claim to fame was being a house painter. BIG mistake bragging about that skill to my mother. My mother's ear perked up. "I just so happen to have some work for you, Mike. I can use both of you to help me."

Early the next morning, about four a.m., my mother, with Josie and Mike in tow, headed to her latest purchase, a century-old Victorian home on the Eastern shore, near Ocean City, Maryland. Twenty-five thousand dollars bought her this eight-bedroom Victorian-style home, two acres of land, and a six-stall horse barn. The Nanticoke River was located across the street from the house.

Rumor had it that a captain of a ship used to live in that house. There was a widow's walk at the very top. Predictably, the house was in very poor shape. Parts of the front porch had fallen in because it had rotted, and the exterior was in desperate need of a coat of paint. Grass and weeds had overtaken the property, and the barn looked like it was about to topple over—not to mention that it was filled with debris and furniture.

The inside of the house was in just as much disrepair. The ceilings were caving in on the second floor from a leaky roof; the hardwood floor had buckled from years of water damage; the leather wallpaper was peeling back; and there were missing tin ceiling tiles on the kitchen ceiling. Dust covered everything. The windows were painted shut, not that it would have made any difference, since most of the windowpanes were broken. Luckily, most of the stained glass panes that decorated each of the window's corners were intact. There was no running water or electricity.

The first winter, my mother and her crew of two mentally ill people lived in that uninhabitable house. They had no heat and no plumbing, and they worked the Mama Moon shift, the one that never ends. They slept approximately four hours a day. "Can't wastee time. Keep working."

Only my mother could have found a way to keep Josie and her boyfriend productive. One day, Josie lost it. She ran out of the house stark naked, screaming at the top of her lungs, "Fuck me! Fuck me!" Now, understand that this was a quiet, subdued neighborhood of retired folks. We hoped most of them were sound asleep when she made her public debut.

My mother frequently had to pick up some supplies at the hardware store, and one time, on her return trip, she brought an unexpected guest back to the Nanticoke house. She hit a deer, whose head ended up through her windshield. I'm not certain if the deer was eye to eye with my mother or if it ended up on the passenger side. My mother sustained some injuries, but according to her, these were not serious enough to warrant medical attention. Nothing short of death would deter her from renovating the Nanticoke home. It didn't turn out all bad either; they did feast on venison.

The entire winter they labored. Victor installed all of the plumbing, and by spring, there was a well, working plumbing, and electricity. We helped out as much as we could. But my time was limited, and so was Victor's. It was a two-and-a-half-hour commute to Nanticoke from Washington, DC.

In the summer, we went to the Nanticoke house to relax. By then, my mother and her crew had finished most of the repairs. Mom had jacked up the wraparound porch and stabilized it with new concrete footers. The house was painted white with black shutters, and the hardwood floors glistened, as did the new tin ceiling in the kitchen. The broken windowpanes had been replaced. Mom had been careful not to damage the original stained glass on the corners of each of the windows. Interior doors were repaired or replaced, and new bathroom fixtures were installed. The barn was repaired and painted.

Almost a year later, my mother and her crew of two completed their work on the Nanticoke house and returned to Arlington. Josie and Mike reoccupied the small one-bedroom bungalow. My mother knew they couldn't afford to pay rent so she planned to employ them until they could get on their feet. She gave them a place to live and gave them food to eat. The odd couple continued to argue, and one day, their argument got out of hand. They took turns throwing one another's clothes in the yard. The next thing, the clothes were on fire. Then the bungalow caught fire.

The couple had worn out their welcome. As much as my mother hated to admit it, she could no longer help them. With nowhere to go, we believed they might have ended up in a homeless shelter. Despite everything, Mom was forever grateful to them for helping her renovate the Nanticoke house.

The burnt bungalow is another story in itself. It wasn't zoned by the county to be a separate house. It probably had started as a shed in the backyard of my mother's first Arlington home. All of a sudden, one day it had an address. I guess my mother decided she wanted another home to rent, with a separate address. Then it had its own electricity and running water. Shortly after, The United States Postal Service started delivering mail there. Mom did whatever she wanted and always seemed to get away with it.

Another similar incident occurred when my mother decided to plant dogwood trees on county property. I told her that she couldn't, but she didn't listen to me. She said, "I make this neighborhood pretty, so the county won't care." The county didn't stop her or they never caught her. So she continued to plant the trees on county property. Now these trees are taller than the utility lines and the county has had to cut back the branches. Sometimes, I wonder if the county questions where these trees came from. If they only knew—decades ago, a hardworking Korean woman planted those trees to make the neighborhood "pretty."

Let's face it, my mother loved to create something out of nothing. Her greatest achievement was the Nanticoke house. It was a real labor of love. Mom promised that our Nanticoke house would be a family home where we could gather. I envisioned the family swimming, eating together, or relaxing on the expansive, wraparound porch and sipping ice-cold lemonade. But I knew that Mom could change her mind in an instant. So I had better not get too enthralled with the "family vacation home."

I don't think my mother saw it the same way. The much-anticipated relaxing summers at Nanticoke turned out to be more like a labor camp.

Victor's younger sister, Nina, came to visit and vacation at the Nanticoke house. I was very close to Nina, as I was to Victor's other sister, Maryanne. We loved their company. Nina was particularly helpful and hardworking. She offered to help do some work around the Nanticoke house. That was a mistake. A big mistake. She didn't know what she was asking for. And of course I couldn't allow Nina to work alone.

My mother asked us to move pile upon pile of assorted wood that she had stored under the porch, where she hoarded building materials. Nina and I moved the wood for six hours. After we finished, we thought that we'd reward ourselves with a nice dip in the water. But before we could go swimming, Mom said, "I changee my mind. Put the wood back under the porch."

That was it. I said, "Enough is enough; we are going swimming." My mother wasn't very happy with my revolt.

***

A year and half after moving in my mother's home, I had finished what I had set out to accomplish; I successfully completed my master's degree. Victor, Jason, and my mother were so proud. I was so relieved! We finally could move out of my mother's house, where a nutty tenant and backbreaking labor awaited us, and move back to our own peaceful home.

My professor asked me what the big hurry was with my completing the program. I just chuckled and thought, *If you only knew about the off-key tenant, the restaurant equipment, and tons of stale motel drapes, you wouldn't need to ask.*

CHAPTER 18

Due to it being near the river, the Nanticoke house needed to be painted again only a year following the extensive renovation. The large eight-bedroom home would require us to give up every weekend in the spring and summer to maintain it. It was also very difficult to maintain two acres of cleared land. We told Mom that she couldn't depend on us to help and to hire a handyman. She said, "I thought my family like this house. If it is too big to take care of on weekend. I sell."

I couldn't help but feel disappointed. She was always changing her mind. She'd voice her good intentions and then decide on a different direction. Like the time she took me car shopping and said that she was planning to buy me a brand-new car to show her appreciation for my years of assistance. I never asked her for such an expensive gift, nor would I ever ask, but I was pleasantly surprised by her generous gesture. At the last minute, she'd find another real estate deal and would change her mind. I wasn't the only one she'd make promises to that she didn't keep.

Mom did the same with Victor when she sold The Country Hut building, after she promised it to Victor. Victor didn't want her to sell The Hut building, as he and my mother had an agreement that if he built up the business, he would own the building in the future. He had invested so much of his time that it was earning a nice profit, and the area was changing rapidly. There were big county plans to build a shopping center and movie theater across the street from the property. Although disappointed that Mom hadn't kept her side of the bargain, Victor didn't protest the sale. He knew, as did I, that once she made up her mind there was no changing it. In his attempt to convince her to hold on to the property, though, he called the corporate headquarters of 7-Eleven, which proposed tearing down the building, erecting a new one, and leasing the building for ten years. The building would produce a positive cash flow and the title would be free and clear in ten years.

My mother eventually sold the Nanticoke house for $120,000 in 1988. Mom earned a handsome profit from the Nanticoke sale in a short period. The new owners successfully applied for the house to be in the historical register, and it was restored to its original pastel colors.

I miss the Nanticoke house to this day. I still have a picture of it in my living room. I wish I had agreed to paint it. But that wouldn't have guaranteed that my mother would have kept it. She was changeable, unpredictable, and headstrong.

Mom reinvested the Nanticoke house proceeds soon after the sale. She didn't want money just lying stagnant in a bank account. Experience had shown her that investing in real estate was much more profitable than a savings account. She liked to invest in property—bricks and mortar. She could see it and feel it. And she took such pride in fixing up old, rundown houses. "Nothing, nothing feels better than to know that these two hands made that old, ugly house pretty."

\*\*\*

Although I had the master's degree, my mother had the business brains. She'd buy where no sane person would, and it would turn out to be a gold mine. A Metro station would appear. Office buildings would sprout. Professionals would replace blue-collar workers. She just knew a good deal when she saw it, or felt it.

A good example of my mother's developed intuition is the time she advised us to purchase thirty acres of unimproved land in Culpeper, Virginia. I'd never heard of the place. When we arrived, I saw farmland and cows. Not much else was going on.

Mom excitedly showed us the land. "It's a good deal," she said. All I saw was an open field and bunch of trees. I asked her why she thought it was such a good deal, and she said that the property was a corner lot and the sun was in a good position. "Can't you feel it? This property makes you feel good."

Although I found her reasoning to be amusing, her successes with real estate were proven. So Victor and I bought the land, although we were not confident of its future value. Just a few months later, we sold the property and doubled our investment. We thought, *That was easy.*

The next month, we bought 114 acres right across the street. We proudly showed my mother our latest purchase. She just shook her head and said, "You people make bad deal." I asked her why she would make such a statement. She replied, "Look—no sun. This is a bad location." That's all she said.

Well, she was right. We couldn't flip the property. So we paid the payments month after month, year after year. Soon they were becoming a financial drain. Finally, after seven years, we sold the land for what we paid for it. I wondered, *How could my mother know?*

CHAPTER 19

My mother needed our help repairing 1 East Luray, her third real estate property, purchased in the early 1970s. My mother was the foreman. Victor, myself, and a few other reluctant relatives made up the construction crew. She needed to repair the place quickly, as she had found a nonprofit group (mostly funded by the government) that wanted to rent the property. This meant she'd have a better chance of receiving timely rent payments.

At the time, I thought the house had to be the most rundown property Mom had ever bought. However, I had thought the same thing every time she bought a property. This house was big, with lots of bedrooms to rent, which met her business model for ensuring she'd make a net profit.

I almost cried when I saw the condition of the place. Would I never get away from this madness? I knew what was in store for us. There went any leisure time I might have had, including time to sleep. Another layer of work to add to my already busy schedule.

As we removed stinky trash and debris, I wondered how people lived like this. Only after a good two weeks of ridding the house of trash were we able to start demolition and repairs. Some of the fixtures we removed and carried out of the house were really heavy: a cast-iron claw-foot tub, heavy sinks, old windows, solid wood doors, and toilets—the good old-fashioned heavy kind. Mom's management style didn't make things any better. Talk about a dictator! She cut us no slack.

My mother would say, "I have a housee payment in one month. I havee to rent this house. We have to finish or I hurtee for money."

But what added to the stress of working for my mother, the dictator, is that she'd change her mind in midstream. "Oh, I changee my mind. I don't want that wall there. Let's tear down and move it over there."

I'd respond, "Mom, what's wrong with the wall where it is?"

She just shook her head. "You don't know anything about fixee up house. You listen to me. This is better. Let's move wall. I don't like talkee back. I'm too tired to talk. Just do it!"

In the middle of the project, Mom lost her car and house keys. She didn't have duplicate keys. We had to find her keys. After unsuccessfully searching, we racked our brains trying to think of places the keys could be. The only place the keys could be was in a deep ditch we had spent all day digging to lay pipe. Mom couldn't wait until the next day for us to recover her keys. Although the sun was starting to set, it had to be done right then. So Victor, me, and one other person dug, while my mother held a flashlight, until we found the keys.

There was no point in trying to reason with her. We'd tear down a day's worth of work and start over. This was a reoccurring theme throughout any project with my mother. Her urgency to finish a task resulted in working by the seat of her pants. Planning made her nervous and slowed things down. This approach mirrored how she lived her life.

For example, she didn't use a map to travel by car. If her instincts couldn't get her to a destination, she'd just stop every mile and ask someone for directions. She'd have to memorize what they said since she couldn't read or write. Then she'd start thinking about the tenant who hadn't paid rent, or the gas company bill, or that she really did want to tear down another wall. She'd forget the directions and need to stop and ask again.

After years of being the obedient daughter, I finally had to put my foot down and tell my mother that I just couldn't work on her rental properties, prepare rental leases and contracts, work full time, and keep my marriage intact. Something had to give. So we agreed that I would resign my construction job with her properties. I continued to do her paperwork—leases, contracts, reading legal agreements, preparing eviction notices and property variances, and such.

My mother seemed unstoppable. If her family refused to help her, she picked up "day laborers"—the chronically unemployed, drug abusers, people on welfare looking to earn some side money, and immigrants hanging out on street corners or at 7-Elevens.

My mother worked side by side with her little crew. She bought them lunch and sodas and sat down with them to eat and talk. Most were pretty good people when you got to know them, although some of her workers had a problem with sticky fingers. My mother would need to use her power drill or her miter box and they would be missing. She found some of her tools in a local pawnshop, where she'd just buy them back.

\*\*\*

My mother was a spectacle in a low-income predominantly black neighborhood. She had no fear of her surroundings or that she was different from everyone else around her. She'd drive up in a fairly new Lincoln Continental, the trunk and back seat filled with paint buckets, tools, and construction materials.

She could be heard throughout the neighborhood, barking orders at her "day laborers" or yelling, "Wake up!" to the unfortunate ones who fell asleep on the job. She could also be heard berating workers for doing "stupid" things, like using flat paint instead of semigloss paint. "You know how to read English; don't be so stupid." She assumed that if *she* knew better, American-raised men should know even more about painting, carpentry, and other stereotypically "male" tasks.

My mother's lack of English skills and general rush to get things done quickly spilled over into how she dealt with county building inspectors. She'd begin building without a building permit, and the building inspectors would catch her, mainly through a visual inspection of the neighborhood or a neighbor. You couldn't blame people for staring.

My mother frequently told me about the mounting pressures of managing the rental properties—finding laborers, the theft of her tools and materials, hassling with building code inspectors, and feuding with neighbors—until my head spun. I didn't know how she could withstand, physically and emotionally, all the pressure.

The building inspectors frequently gave her citations for violating county building codes. She would have to stop work on repairing her properties and try to comply with the county. Normally, I would complete the building permit application and other paperwork that was required, but if she couldn't find me, she'd ask one of her labors to complete the building permit application. Most of her laborers had no idea how to fill in the application.

"Miss Moon, I dunno how to write this. I sorry."

My mother would be shocked. "Whatza matter with you? You born in United States and you don't know how to write? It simple. Just do."

Sometimes they would attempt to fill out the paperwork, and of course, the county would reject the application and my mother would have to start over.

She may have had difficulty learning how to read and write—but she instinctively knew how to draw. She drew up the building plans, which passed inspection with flying colors.

But then she ran into problems with neighbors on adjacent properties. One neighbor sued her for destroying a stone wall that was on the property line. The neighbor claimed that my mother's excavation caused the wall to crack.

Mom hired a soil engineer and structural engineer to prove that the wall had been structurally unstable for a number of years. The neighbor was eligible for legal aid, while my mother had to pay lawyers, engineers, and witness wage losses—all because she worked and could afford to. It just didn't seem fair since the neighbor's claim had no merit. The wall had significant cracks when my mother bought the property.

When Mom finished repairing these homes, she preferred renting to families who received government rental assistance. By receiving rental payments from the government, she could relax, knowing she'd receive payments on time. After a while, the people in the community where she owned low-income rental properties grew to respect my mother, and Mom became fond of many of the people in the community. They saw how hard she worked on the properties; painting, repairing, and cleaning the yards. Mom would tell me they'd be walking by her property and shaking their heads. "I've never seen a woman work so hard in all of my life."

Mom also tried to help needy families in the community by donating clothes, food, and money, and helping them find jobs. She'd even give them free advice. Individuals thanked Mom for helping them stop the welfare cycle that had been a part of their family for generations. Mom's stories resonated with many to whom she shared the obstacles she'd overcome. She inspired them to work hard, so that they too could be self-sufficient one day. They fondly called my mother, mama Moon.

After seeing Americans live in poverty, Mom thanked God she had a strong body and mind with which to overcome obstacles and work even harder. She didn't think it possible to be poor in America.

Other times, Mom became dejected about not pampering herself. She'd say, "Sujan, sometimes I think I not a woman. How can I work so hard? I just like a man. Sometimes, I ashamed to wear these dirty clothes."

One time she became so angry for not spending on herself, she drove to a fur store in the clothes she wore while painting a house. When the clerk saw her walk in the store, she turned up her nose. Not knowing what to say to Mom, she pretended she didn't exist. Mom walked to the counter, plopped down a brown paper bag on it, and pulled out ten thousand dollars. She pointed to a mink coat. When the store clerk saw the cash, she couldn't wait on her fast enough.

CHAPTER 20

In 1987 Woon Gee's and his wife's marriage was legally dissolved, however, his marriage ended much earlier. My mother didn't fault her former daughter-in-law for leaving him. She knew far too well what she was feeling: trapped, stripped of her self-esteem, and beaten into submission. Despite Mom's disappointment in her son, she supported him financially during and following the breakup of his marriage. My mother felt responsible for her son's behavior, so she also assisted her ex-daughter-in-law in starting a new life by purchasing her a bustling food carryout business in a commercial office building in the heart of Rosslyn, Virginia.

Woon Gee was dating a Korean woman. He may have found happiness, but it was short-lived. About two weeks before Christmas Day, in 1988, Woon Gee was brutally murdered at age thirty-nine, three months shy of his fortieth birthday.

I'm not certain I'll ever know the entire truth about the facts of his murder. I'd heard that he was dating a younger Korean woman whose brother objected to the relationship. Despite the brother's protest, they intended to marry. The brother was at Woon Gee's apartment when an argument ensued about Woon Gee's relationship with his sister. Rumor was that they had been drinking alcohol. In their drunken state, the argument escalated to a fistfight, the brother grabbed a butcher knife from the kitchen, and fatally stabbed Woon Gee.

Hearing that the murderer was planning to escape to Korea, we informed the police, who said not to worry because they had all airports covered. They were wrong. He escaped on an airplane headed to Korea. I heard he departed from Dulles Airport, approximately a thirty-minute drive from the murder scene.

\*\*\*

Mom asked Victor and me to go to Woon Gee's apartment to clean and remove his personal belongings. We reluctantly went, not knowing what to expect. We entered his apartment, greeted by a horrific scene.

I had expected to see blood. But I wasn't prepared for what looked like large pieces of bloody liver, in varying sizes, staining Woon Gee's brown couch and parquet floor. I later learned that the blood had coagulated, turning the pools of blood into gell. There was a strong stench, like rotting steak.

Judging from the disarray of the apartment's furnishings, the coffee table lying on its side, couch cushions strewn around; it appeared that there was quite a struggle between the murderer and Woon Gee. From the blood trail, it seemed Woon Gee intially bled on the couch, and then fell to the floor, knocking over the coffee table. Most of the blood was on the floor where he may have bled to death.

We were astounded that the apartment's property manager and law enforcement officials had allowed us, relatives of the deceased person, to witness the brutality of the murder. The scene was far too gruesome for us to remain in the apartment. We told the property manager to keep Woon Gee's security deposit to pay for the cleaning service.

My mother, even in her shocked, grief-stricken state, couldn't stand wasting anything. She insisted that we pick up Woon Gee's dining room set. "It is in good shape; I can use." I was horrified that she could eat on the table that was part of a murder scene—and not only a murder scene, but the bloody, gruesome murder of her son.

I understood my mother and accepted her unconventional ways, but I didn't think my husband could understand why she would want us to return to the scene of the murder to retrieve a cheap dining room set which she didn't need. I knew she had endured so much hardship in her life that it was impossible for her to waste anything, so this made perfect sense to me, although I wished she'd quit living in the past.

In the end, my mother got her way. Victor didn't want me to return to the apartment, so he had a couple of friends help him move the dining room set. The table was made of stone, faux marble, and was extremely heavy. He and his friends couldn't maneuver it through the entrance door, so they had to lower it from the balcony. Nothing was easy when it came to my mother. Regardless, if she wanted it, she expected people to find a way to make it happen.

## CHAPTER 21

How much pain can one human being endure? My mother fought the demons that seemed to follow her. Starting with losing Ed, the love of her life. Her beloved baby daughter. Dependable Frank. Her eldest son. The suddenness of these unexpected losses cut deep in her soul. How could she trust what the next day would bring?

Although she remained strong in her mind, her body was taking a beating. She became sickly. Nevertheless, she tried to fight her physical deterioration, making a concerted effort not to walk with a limp, although her leg felt like burning hot mush. She would stand up straight, even though her spine wanted to curve because of bone loss. Nevertheless she continued to tend to her yard, work on her rental properties, and look for good business deals.

However, her biggest sorrow was greater than all the deaths and losses combined. It was something that she was powerless to stop. It invaded every bone in her body. She tried everything to fix it: prayer, screaming, threatening. If anyone could make someone change out of sheer willpower, it was my mother, but nothing seemed to change this situation.

Mom and I remained hopeful that Eddie would overcome his drug addiction and grow up to be a responsible adult. But Eddie, at age thirty, was still shooting up drugs and living with Mom. He had no job. No ambition. No dreams. He was just hanging on to life for his next hit of crack cocaine. If my mother hadn't financially supported him, he would have been one of the faceless homeless men you'd see wandering the city streets or sleeping on heating grates.

Eddie stole from my mother. She showed me copies of the checks he forged. He even pawned her valuables. She had to lock up her money, jewelry, tools—anything she didn't want Eddie to pawn. She was constantly hiding money and jewelry until she forgot where she hid things. Then she would go crazy looking for whatever she had hidden. When she couldn't find the lost item, she was never sure if she'd lost it or if Eddie had stolen it. That was the way she lived, year after year after year.

My mother tried keeping her valuables locked in every type of safe, but Eddie could open just about any lock. He was "smart in stupid ways," as she would say. He found it amusing to crack safes. It would just reinforce how brilliant he thought he was.

Finally, one incident occurred that I thought was the last straw. Perhaps she'd quit enabling him and force him to be accountable for himself. Mom was going to settle on a property she had purchased but found, to her horror, that her checking account was overdrawn. Eddie had managed to forge ten thousand dollars in checks, over a period of a week or so. The bank said that it would redeposit the funds in her checking account if she'd press criminal charges against her son. Mom refused because she didn't want Eddie to have a criminal record, although he was already a felon. She believed he would change eventually.

When I asked Eddie how he could hurt our mother repeatedly if he loved her, he would just shrug his shoulders and say, "I dunno. I'll change. I won't do it again." After years of hearing the same old broken record, I concluded that he was a sociopath, incapable of feeling remorse. I heard that he spent the money at Ocean City, Maryland, partying with friends.

Eddie continued to lie and steal from my mother, but she never gave up on him. She even went as far as to try to see why my brother got such a thrill from drugs by watching him shoot up. One night, she crouched behind a living room chair, hiding, and waiting in the dark living room for Eddie. Like a creepy night creature, Eddie would sleep during the day and stay awake all night.

Eddie lit a match under a bent teaspoon used to heat up the drug, laying it and a syringe on the coffee table so his hands were free to tie a tourniquet around his arm. My mother watched as her beloved son stuck the syringe needle in his swollen vein. As the drug surged through his body, a sound of satisfaction escaped his lips.

My mother couldn't hold back her emotion and horror at what she was witnessing. Eddie heard her muffled cry and turned on the lamp. My mother, crouched behind an overstuffed chair, head bowed, hands clasped, tears streaming down her cheeks, emitted sounds of pain that only a mother can feel. Eddie simply turned and walked out of the living room. No words were exchanged.

As a mother myself, I can feel the pain Eddie has caused my mother. I hated the cause of Mom's pain. Why wouldn't Eddie just go away and allow Mom to live a peaceful life? What purpose did he serve?

When Eddie told me this story, a pain shot through the core of my body, as if I were present and it happened just yesterday. Even Eddie, in his drug-induced state, understood he caused Mom heartache but he felt too helpless to do anything about it. He wrote, years later, "I'd hear Mom crying and praying for me every night."

Eventually, Mom feared she might kill my brother as he continued to steal, lie, and take drugs. I would tell her to kick him out of her home and her life if that was the way she felt. There was no point in her suffering. He was an adult who seemed perfectly happy with his life. Then Mom would direct her anger at me. "You cold fish. No feeling for your brother. No matter what, he your brother."

Mom didn't kill my brother, but she'd beat him with her fist or pummel him with the nearest object at hand, all the while shouting at him, "My Eddie, how can you hurt your mother like this?" He hardly felt anything in his drug-induced state; he'd just escape to another room or hold my mother's arms so she couldn't hit him. These situations usually ended with Mom sobbing and collapsing from exhaustion.

Her health continued to decline, and I believe her stressful life was the cause of her illness. One day, she'd be in bed sick; the next day, painting a house.

Mom didn't want to bother me with her illness, so she didn't tell me about a particularly bad illness. I found out later that one of her male construction workers took care of her while she was ill, going so far as to assist her to the bathroom and feed her until she regained her health. To my mother, survival was king. Modesty was for the weak. You did what you had to do to survive, as long as you weren't lying, stealing, or killing. Basically, obey God's Ten Commandments. She'd say, "Who cares about what other people think?"

When I discovered how ill my mother had been, Victor and I decided to move closer to her. I felt bad that I had been too busy to notice. In July 1989, we bought the home in which my mother was living. She moved across the street, back to our very first home in Arlington.

*\*\**

My mother wanted a big house. A really big house. She had always planned on moving to a big house when she remarried. At age fifty-seven, she didn't see much chance of marrying again. How could she ever trust a man again? Suppose someone wanted to marry her for her money?

My mother submitted the plans to build an approximately nine-thousand-square-foot house in place of the less than two-thousand-square-foot home. The county zoning department rejected her building plans because the house's boundaries were too close to the neighbor's property line.

However, my mother never took "no" for an answer. She hung around the zoning department asking questions to anyone willing to assist her. Some people felt sorry for the illiterate Korean woman trying to navigate zoning. Others thought she was a nuisance. She'd approach county personnel, contractors, whoever she believed could read and write English. She still hadn't mastered the English language, so she had to rely on anyone who was patient enough to teach her the ropes. She simply would not give up.

Mom's perseverance finally paid off. She found a way around the zoning regulations. House boundaries were not as strict for house *additions*, so rather than tearing down and building a new home, my mother added approximately seven thousand square feet to the existing house. It worked. Her building plans passed zoning. Armed with a building permit, my mother was once again ready to put on her foreman's hard hat.

She wanted the addition to look like part of the house, and she liked all-brick homes. The existing home's exterior was siding. Since she could not tear down the existing home, she bricked right over it.

She ended up with eight bedrooms on the first two levels of the house; seven bedrooms on the second floor, of which three bedrooms were master bedroom size, and one master bedroom on the first floor. She also installed seven bathrooms, a one-to-one ratio between bedrooms and bathrooms.

That wasn't enough. She built out the large attic area by installing a kitchen area and two bedrooms. She rented the space as a little apartment.

And it didn't end there. She built out the basement on the addition, creating a family room with a nice fireplace, which looked as big as a football field. Another kitchen area and two more bedrooms were added, and another apartment was listed for rent in the classified ads.

Recall my description of the old basement of the first house we bought in Arlington: low ceilings, small. It's the house we spent our summer digging out another room. Well, my mother rented that space, too. Of course, the tenants had to be short or risk being knocked out by the plumbing pipes running across the ceiling. That covered the basement, first floor, second floor, and attic.

But wait, there is more. She found more wasted space: the garage. Why use that big space for a car? There were better uses. She built a loft, which she turned into a laundry room and storage area. She cut a doorway from the kitchen to the new laundry/storage area. To enter the storage area, you had to bend way down.

The county building inspectors discovered that the fireplace exterior extended a few inches past the appropriate boundary. To tear down the fireplace would be expensive. To avoid doing so, Mom sought a zoning variance. I had to attend the variance meeting to speak on Mom's behalf. I didn't feel comfortable being in the spotlight in what turned out to be a controversial issue. Neighbors didn't like the largeness of my mother's home and didn't want her operating a "boarding house."

Mom also managed to anger the neighbor who lived next door to Victor and me. One day as I drove my car in our driveway, I saw my neighbor hugging a tree stump, crying and very upset. I walked over to the chain-link fence separating our properties alongside the driveway. I asked her what was wrong. She angrily responded that my mother had cut down her trees, pointing to the seven or more tree stumps that lined the chain-link fence.

The neighbor said that earlier she had given Mom permission to pick the mulberries from the trees, not cut them down. I tried to explain that my mother had an English language handicap. The neighbor didn't believe me, because she said that my mother couldn't own a big house across the street without the ability to understand English. The neighbor said that she bought the house because she loved the mature trees that lined our driveway. I felt so ashamed and bad for our neighbor. To top it off, I heard that the neighbor worked for the Environmental Protection Agency.

I quickly ran in the house and told Victor that Mom had cut down our neighbor's trees. Victor turned white, then red with rage. He knew Mom was capable of this. He was so embarrassed that he didn't want to walk out our front door, in fear the neighbor would see him. Now I had Victor and the neighbor upset with me.

I was so angry with my mother I was boiling. I wouldn't hold back this time. Years of pent-up anger came spilling out when I finally confronted her. My mother became very upset, seeing me so upset, especially since I normally kept my emotions in check.

Mom said that she did ask the neighbor's permission to cut down the mulberry trees. She attempted to explain to the neighbor that the mulberries from the tree limbs, which hung over our driveway, were staining it and our carpets from people tracking in mulberry juice on the soles of their shoes.

She did not acknowledge any wrongdoing. Mom thought she was right. She had asked permission and received it—so what's the big deal? Besides, Mom said, the trees were ugly and she'd replace them with nicer trees. That statement just made me angrier. I tried to explain that just because she didn't think something was attractive didn't mean others saw it that way.

The next day the neighbor contacted a tree expert, which I suspected was the first step toward taking legal action. I was anxious as I calculated the expenses for an attorney and replacement trees, all while trying to finance a George Washington doctoral program, which I had started a few years back. My mother had someone transcribe an elementary level apology note to the neighbor, stating that she had never seen me (her daughter) so upset. I doubt if the note had any impact on the neighbor forgiving us, because to this day, the neighbor has not spoken a word to me. She also did not take legal action.

Some neighbors looked for ways to prevent my mother from constructing the large house addition. In fact, an article ran in the local paper, headlined "Monster House Invades Neighborhood." My mother was very proud. I tried to explain to her that the article wasn't flattering. She didn't care.

At the variance meeting, a debate ensued between two individuals on the county variance board. The person opposed to Mom's addition was an older white male. The person who tried to exercise fairness was a younger black male. The white male commented that Mom's house looked like an apartment building, garnering a few chuckles from the hearing's attendees. I was embarrassed. My mother smiled broadly. The black male reminded the council that Mom had followed all county guidelines, and that the purpose of the meeting wasn't to judge whether neighbors liked the size or appearance of her home.

From where I sat, I believed that he, being a minority, understood how it felt to be different. He went on to say that the contractor made an innocent mistake and that he wanted the council to consider that the error would have no impact on the adjacent neighbor, since the fireplace didn't cross Mom's property line. In the end, the variance was approved; Mom didn't have to tear down the fireplace.

***

Mom was the subcontractor for all of her home repairs. She earned the respect of construction workers. A constant theme from them was, "Damn, I ain't ever seen a woman work as hard as she does. Man, does she stay on our back. But she's a good woman. She treats me like a mother. Tells me how to straighten up my life. Gives me good advice. And she a good cook, too."

At dinnertime, I've frequently seen my mother sitting at her kitchen table, eating and telling jokes with her workers in her broken English. His-panic, African American—it made no difference to her. Only one thing mat-tered: a good work ethic. If you worked hard, you were okay in her book.

It seemed like in no time at all, although I imagine it had to take years, the house was complete. My mother and my brother moved into the house. Mom was optimistic that with a fresh start in a "brand-new" home, Eddie would straighten up, find a good woman to marry, have children, and open a business. They could all live happily ever after in the same house. She gave Eddie a nice big master bedroom, decorating it and buy-ing nice bedroom furniture for him, as if he were a normal functioning and loving son—a son who would take care of his mother, like all good Korean sons.

It wasn't too long before my mother recognized that a nice home wasn't going to change Eddie. He lived like a pig—well, like a drug ad-dict. Clothes were strewn everywhere. Dirty dishes, half-filled glasses, and rotting food covered the furniture, the floor, the window ledges, and the bathroom.

It drove my mother crazy thinking about my brother holed up in his bedroom shooting drugs into his veins. His drug buddies would join him in his brand-new bedroom. There was no telling what else they were up to.

Finally, Mom had enough. She moved Eddie downstairs into the fam-ily room where she could keep an eye on him. She also could chase away his drug buddies; the glass French doors didn't provide much privacy. Of course, Eddie covered them up with blankets and sheets, which my mother would tear down, all the while cursing in Korean.

Since my brother now occupied the family room, my mother decided to convert the deck to an enclosed space where she could sew and store more stuff. I asked her why she would want to ruin the house. She had used up almost every square inch of yard space to build her addition, and now she wanted to enclose the small space that remained to entertain outdoors. It just didn't make a bit of sense. Did she really need another room?

Mom told me to "shut my mouth" and did what she set out to do. She used extremely heavy commercial windows to enclose the porch. The heavy glass, encased in metal, served as the frame and support for the walls and roof. She even found old skylights for the new room. They look like the plastic domes covering bus stops. The deck's foundation wasn't built to support an enclosed room, especially one that was so heavy, but the safety issue didn't seem to concern my mother.

One day, while Mom was making some final touches on the outside of the newly enclosed deck, she accidently fell, headfirst, down a seven-foot concrete stairwell, which led to the home's basement. When her head initially hit the concrete landing, she said that her first thought was, *Did I die?* Quickly recovering from the shock of the painful fall, she was in disbelief that she could actually stand up. She was lucky to have survived such a forceful impact to her head. Although her head had deep lacerations, her body bruised and sore, and her back injured, my mother was grateful that she had escaped death once again.

When she finished the room, she was so proud of herself. "I usee old commercial store window I keep, even shower door. I even use ceiling fan I buy on sale many years ago. I build wonderful, sunny room." She moved her sewing machine into the room, and gradually other stuff piled up. The thick glass enclosure with skylights created a very hot room. Lucky for her, she liked hot weather. If you added water, the new room could have been a sauna, although it was useless when the weather turned cold.

When Mom had completely settled into her new (but old) home, she was using every square inch of the house as productively as possible. The home was very impressive, considering my mother was leading the charge in her ever-changing way. Her communication skills had caused many a misunderstanding and plenty of arguments with the subcontractors. Somehow, through it all, she managed to build her dream home.

While working on building her home, she also was trying to achieve another important goal: to learn how to write in the English language and grow closer to God. Although her sister's husband and son-in-law were ministers, they didn't take the time to minister to her. Only the Jehovah's Witnesses came to her home every week, so she grew close to the humble people of that faith. She had grown tired of the hypocrisy she witnessed at church, where she'd hear people bragging about their worldly goods or gossiping about other parishioners. Jehovah's Witnesses spoke from the heart as they patiently taught Mom the tenets of their religion.

At the same time, Mom was transcribing the entire Bible in both English and Korean, with the goal of understanding the King James Version and improving her English language skills. Years later, she finished the daunting task. Unfortunately, copying words in English, without an understanding of sentence structure, didn't improve Mom's English language abilities.

CHAPTER 22

My mother would drive me crazy lending money to Korean business owners and family. With no legal agreement, she would hand over hundreds of thousands of dollars on a promise and a handshake. Over my protests, she would say, "We trust each other. Don't need a piece of paper. That's the way Korean people do business."

Mom was royally ripped off at times. She didn't see it that way. "Sometimes people can't pay it back right away. They pay later." Or she would lend them more money to make money in order to repay the loan. "If I don't help them, they can't pay me back." In many instances, her reasoning actually worked.

I recall an incident when a Korean businessperson, who I will call Ms. No, borrowed a substantial amount of money from my mother. I was never certain of the exact amount, but I heard it was well over a million bucks. Ms. No was highly respected in the Korean community for her network and thriving businesses. She owned a real estate company and a mortgage company.

It was handy that the two businesses were located next to one another: get approval for a mortgage, then simply walk next door, where Ms. No would line you up with a home or business. She always found creative ways to qualify newly immigrated Koreans for homes and businesses.

Ms. No would pull into my mother's driveway in her new shining Mercedes-Benz. She always looked put together, with an expensive, pressed suit, a diamond ring, and nice earrings. Her makeup was flawless. Her hair was always well groomed, not a hair out of place. She always looked professional and successful, smiling and confident.

Ms. No even decorated her businesses to look successful. The rugs were green—the color of money. She once told me that you had to behave as if you are successful before you can be. Yes, I believe I've heard that line on infomercials promoting get rich quick schemes.

Most of the time my mother would meet with Ms. No at home, where my mother conducted most of her business. On most days, Mom wasn't concerned with appearances. She'd greet Ms. No in her nightgown and robe or paint-crusted work clothes. But then, occasionally she'd be in a suit. Sometimes you couldn't tell if she was ready to retire to bed or conduct business.

Stories of my mother's dress style, or lack of, spread among the more malicious Korean women, who would make fun of her and call her a *coogee*, the Korean word for beggar—although my mother had helped many of these same women financially.

"Moon, you can afford nice clothes; you can afford to eat at good restaurants, and take nice vacations. Why are you working like a man? Why are you wearing men's clothes, with your fingernails broken and dirty?" her so-called friends would say repeatedly, as if trying to be helpful. My mother would be upset to the point of crying after such comments. She knew she was the butt of many jokes about her frugal ways among the Koreans.

She would tell me, "When I die, people will laugh at me and ask if I took my money with me. I poor when I was young. I starve in war. I don't know how to waste." I would try to comfort her. "Mom, they're coming to your house to borrow money. The reason you have money is that you've saved your money. They're spending more money than they can afford." My mother would respond, "Yeah they just show off. I not like those people. I no wastee money."

When Koreans had a financial need, though, they would try to brown-nose my mother—even the ones who were jealous of her, the ones who couldn't accept the fact that my mother had earned every dime she had accumulated, without a college degree. They swore that a man had given her the money, possibly that Sergeant Garza "character." As time went on, Koreans passed rumors that several men were financially supporting my mother. If there were several men, Mom did an excellent job of hiding them from me.

I was at her home a couple of times when Ms. No came to do business. After listening to them discuss the terms and conditions of a loan of hundreds of thousands of dollars, I said to Ms. No, "This latest business venture seems pretty risky to my mother. I don't see you taking any risks." Ms. No laughed and said, "Everything is a risk. That's business." My mother nodded in agreement. I just walked out of the house, thinking, *These people are nuts.*

A few months later, my mother came to my home in tears. She was visibly shaking when she confided in me, "I don't want to tell you because you get mad at me. I'm so stupid. I lend all my money to Ms. No. She have big problems. She cannot pay me back."

I felt like shouting, *I knew it would happen! Why can't you ever listen to me?* But I didn't say anything, because I knew it wouldn't help matters.

I heard through the grapevine that Ms. No was "borrowing from Peter to pay Paul." She would lend Koreans money from her mortgage company and ask them if they would borrow a little extra for her to use. I also heard that she would use her clients' escrow money and house sale proceeds for her personal use, most likely trying to pay her debts. The most tragic rumor was that of a Korean who was so distraught over losing his life savings to Ms. No that he went to her real estate office and murdered her brother.

My mother could forgive the most unworthy people. She didn't blame Ms. No for taking just about everything she had worked so hard to acquire. My mother said that they had years when they had a good business relationship, and that if Ms. No could have paid her back, she would have. In fact, if she had more money to lend, she would have done so to help Ms. No get out of her business mess. Instead of dwelling on defeat, my mother focused on how to rebuild her financial nest egg.

After this, Mom was a little more cautious when she lent money to a particular Korean she didn't fully trust. She secured the woman's home, and her intuition paid off. The woman defaulted on a fifty-thousand-dollar loan and my mother took title of her home. She had to invest another fifty thousand to pay off the mortgage, but she felt in the end that the equity in the home would increase. That way, she could reclaim her investment. It did work out as she planned, in the longer run.

\*\*\*

My mother's big comfortable renovated home, the one where we lived when we first moved to Arlington, where she had first learned about earning a living as a property manager, would be her key to rebuilding what she had lost to Ms. No. She began building little bedrooms throughout the house. Her family room became two bedrooms. Her enclosed front porch became another bedroom. My mother opened her house to people who were loners. They didn't seem to have any family or friends; at least, I never witnessed that they received any letters or phone calls. They seemed to be the abandoned. Some were alcoholics or had lost everything to alcohol abuse in their past.

Mom would try to help tenants when she thought they had promise or if they had been kind to her. I recall a tenant who was an attorney with a law degree from Georgetown University. My mother saw so much potential in him and couldn't comprehend why he would want to throw away his education and career for a life of alcoholism. She worked particularly hard to turn him around, and eventually he did stop drinking. I can't say whether she had anything to do with it, but I'd like to think she made a difference in his life.

Then there was a retired government executive, Mr. Thurm. He rented a bedroom from my mother for decades, renting elsewhere for a few years after Eddie stole the gun he used to carry out his duties at a part-time security job. He was very nice in a peculiar way. He was tall and thin. He always wore a clean but tattered dress shirt and a suit. Mom would comment, "Even I would throw away some of the clothes Mr. Thurm wears." She'd buy him a shirt, coat, whatever she found on sale. So what if he had seventy-five pairs of old stinky shoes? Or seemingly saved every newspaper he ever read, which were stacked from the floor to the ceiling in his bedroom.

Not once did I observe Mr. Thurm receiving a personal letter or phone call during the entire time I knew him. Although he was a loner, he would visit with my mother. He would read my mother's mail aloud to her. He also never turned down a meal, regardless of how hot and spicy it was. He would make noises while he ate—um, um, um.

My mother was grateful for Mr. Thurm being a good tenant for many years and his willingness to read her mail to her. He even lent her money once, with interest, of course. She wasn't one to just voice her appreciation. When Mr. Thurm became ill and bedridden, my mother fed him in bed, bathed him, and cared for him.

It was apparent that my mother wasn't physically able to care for Mr. Thurm as his physical dependency increased. Mom's own health was failing—years earlier the Social Security Administration certified my mother disabled after reviewing her medical history. That was news to my mother. After all, she was still able to move about. She received disability payments coinciding with her past medical records. My mother was ecstatic. She called me on the phone and said, "Sujan, this country is wonderful. They give me 'back pay.' I get Social Security check and I can still walk." It was a small sum of money, but she was grateful.

Mom asked one of her construction crew to help her lift Mr. Thurm and place him in the bathtub. A sponge bath can only go so far. Thus, I was delighted to discover when reviewing Mr. Thurm's mail that he had long-term care insurance. We secured a nursing home for him, where my mother visited Mr. Thurm several times a week until he died in August 1999.

Another time, I was eating breakfast at my mother's home when a sleepy-eyed, yawning, young Hispanic man entered the kitchen area through the laundry room door. His entrance startled me, since I hadn't expected to see someone emerging from the laundry room. I asked Mom where he came from. She said that he was helping her repair her properties. Without a place to live, she offered him the attic area above the garage, which only could be accessed through the laundry room. He had to bend over when in the space since it wasn't tall enough to walk upright. Mom had also rigged up electricity, so he had lights, heat, and a working television. As I've said throughout, my mother didn't waste a square inch of her large home.

I would tell my mother that she had enough money to be comfortable, despite the money she'd lost to Ms. No. She should live comfortably and get these weird people out of her house. She said, "These people are just like you and me. They had hard life. They help me more than my family does." It was just that simple to her. She didn't think they were beneath her. They were just people, like you and me, trying to live life as best they could.

## CHAPTER 23

Victor breaks the silence. "We're almost there. See, there's the hospital."

I snap back to the present, feeling like I've been in a fog. I'm so grateful that I have been able to focus on something other than what I am about to face. *My mother, my independent mother, how will she be able to live in a wheelchair? My mother, my beautiful mother, what will she say when she sees her scarred, burned face for the first time?*

We enter the hospital and sit in a small waiting room. Some time passes, I have no idea how much; then I glance up to see a doctor in the doorway. "Mrs. Gayle, you can see your mother."

I glance at my watch. "It's six a.m.," I say to no one in particular. Victor is sitting by my side on the vinyl hospital couch. We slowly rise. I want to see. I don't want to see. I hear the doctor steadily walking behind us, quietly instructing us where to go.

I enter her room. Bandages cover her from head to toe. She looks like a mummy. I sit down beside her in a chair next to the bed, and just look at her. Tubes and IVs are doing their job. I think, *Pretty soon she'll be on her own. Just like she would want.*

I look up at the doctor. "When do you think she'll be released?"

He looks surprised. I'm not certain why. I ask again, "When do you think she'll be released?"

He walks toward me. My heart starts beating harder, harder. I don't understand. *What am I dreading? She'll be okay. I just know it. She's beaten every dreadful disease and illness.*

The doctor says, "Your mother is not leaving this hospital alive. She won't get better. Ninety-five percent of her body was burned."

I'm silent.

I stare at nothing.

Thoughts start buzzing around in my head. The noise gets louder and louder. It feels like a bomb just went off in my head.

Beating, beating, beating. *That's my heart. Okay, that is my heart. What's going on with me?*

I think. I look at my mom lying there, covered in gauze, which is white except where blood is seeping through. Her fingers peek out of the gauze. They look like little Italian sausages bursting at the seams. *How can those be her hands?*

The doctor said that they had to slice her here and there. If they didn't, she would burst. I think, *Just like a sausage cooking. You know it's well cooked when the skin can't hold the juices and expanding meat inside the casing.*

This is worse than a horror flick.

What's especially disturbing is that I'm the main character. I'm the mad scientist. I'd have to be crazy to have one coherent thought running through my head. I'd have to be mad to be able to keep sitting here. In this chair. Next to my burnt mother. *Why am I not just falling over with grief? Why does my heart keep beating?* This is more than I can bear.

My mother with cooked organs.

I stare at her.

That's my mother lying in that bed. Not some stranger. My precious mother. Bent over in her flower garden, glancing up when she sees me, big smile, waving at me with love in her eyes. Sunshine everywhere. The flowers she's cared for smile up at their caretaker.

That's my mother. Wrapped like a mummy, bursting out of her own skin, just like a sausage. *She's not a sausage!* I scream to myself. The scientist begins taking mental notes.

*I can't see her arms. I can't see her legs. I can't see her chest. Her eyes are covered with two lumps of gauze.* Lump triggers a thought. *Didn't they put coal on the eyes of the dead to keep their lids shut?* But she's not dead.

I reach a very scientific conclusion. The mad scientist makes up her mind. *She has a chance. MDs aren't always right. She's a miracle. She'll have a rough life. But she's a strong woman. She'll make it. Somehow, she'll survive. Just like she always has.*

*My mother is a fighter. My mother is a winner.*

*Winners always come out on top. Or do they? Can anyone win in the end? Or is dying really winning? Who knows? Who cares?*

*Yep. She'll make it. With cooked organs and all.*

Another person emerges in my head. She's screaming. *God, my head hurts. Stop screaming. I can't take it.*

This isn't happening. Not to me, a normal, average person. This only happens to other people. This day isn't any different from any other day. Not too long ago, Victor and I were just a married couple taking a ride in our car. In one second, less than one second, we entered the realm of horror.

A third person emerges in my mind—and just in time. She's the highly efficient manager. Very organized. *Let's give 'er a big bonus for getting this under control.* Thoughts become more linear, giving the false impression that things are under control.

*Now let's make sense out of this. The MD said she isn't going to make it. Well, if that's true, why did hospital personnel bother to wrap her carefully in gauze? If she wasn't going to make it, why did they bother with inserting all those IVs? If she didn't have a chance, why is she hooked up to a ventilator? If she wasn't going to make it, then why the hell did the doctors make me believe that she would?*

Or did they?

*What is the point of her lying here, being cared for by some of the best medical practitioners? Why?* I shake my head and lower my eyes in order to focus better, to try to get my thoughts back together.

*Why me? Why anyone? I don't understand. "It's not for you to understand, child. It's God's greater plan." Who said that? God? Oh boy, that commentary really made me feel much better. Let's go bury her.*

*Any other great words of wisdom out there? Oh yes, Kübler-Ross. The stages of grieving. Let's see if I can recall. Denial, anger, and acceptance. Okay, that doesn't make me feel better. Big deal. I recognize that I may be going through the stages of grieving.*

*Isn't there anything else out there that can help me make sense of this? Any other words of wisdom? I am grasping at straws. I need something to help me make sense of this.*

*Perhaps a guardian angel will appear and comfort me.*

No angel appears.

*Go to hell, angel. If I ever needed you, it's now. Where are you?*

Finally, I have to accept the news.

I break. I finally break. The mad scientist has deserted me. The efficient manager has receded. My guardian angel didn't come through.

I cry.

I weep.

Every bone. Every organ. My skin. In unison, they cry.

*Why this way? Cooked. Why cooked?*

*What happened to dying peacefully in her bed? How about a massive heart attack? Or cancer? Or a car accident? Or all of the above?*

*Why cooked? What did she do to deserve this?*

"Take off her bandages from her eyes," I say to the doctor.

They are removed.

I stare.

She stares back.

"Please, close her eyes," I say.

The doctor can't seem to find the words.

"Please close her eyes," I say again. This time my voice is louder. I must have known. But that old friend, denial, was trying to help me.

"We can't close her eyes," the doctor says.

"Why not?"

"She doesn't have any eyelids."

Glazed burnt eyes staring back at me. No lids. No eyelashes. Just eyeballs in sockets. Staring.

The doctors begin unwinding the gauze on her head. Her face looks like a monster's. Swollen, blackened, like a well-done steak. Cooked. Yes, she is well done. There are bloody, stiff, burnt patches of hair.

It's unbelievable. I'm standing next to a hospital bed where my cooked mother is dying. Past tense, dead. Or did she die? The ventilator is keeping her alive.

*How can I bear it? It's amazing what you can endure. But can I? Time will tell.*

Her looks were important to her. She couldn't even leave this earth with her good looks. Well, she got her wish. She didn't want to grow old. At least, she didn't want to look or feel old, the reason she underwent plastic surgery last year. She wouldn't want to waste money on something that didn't last for a long, long time. But at least she won't need another face-lift where she's going. That's for sure.

*Poor, poor Mama Moon. Why did you have to go through this?*

I bend over, toward her ear. Her poor, bloody, burnt ears. They are still covered with gauze. Perhaps I am whispering in a hole that used to look like an ear.

She's a fighter. "I love you, Mom," I softly whisper. "Let go, you can quit now. You've struggled enough. I love you more than you'll ever know."

"Please, identify your mother's husband," the doctor says.

Victor and I follow the doctor. I'm afraid that I won't be with my mother when her soul finally leaves her broken-down, burnt body.

*When will this nightmare end? How can I ever erase these images?* They are now imprinted in my psyche.

Artulo, my mother's husband of one year, is lying very peacefully in a hospital bed. His head is swollen, barely recognizable; it looks at least five times larger in diameter. His skin is stretched around a swollen skull, brain tissue expanded with nowhere to go. His eyes, nose, and mouth, distorted on a blackened canvas. I stare at him. His swollen head looks like a jack-o'-lantern.

"Yes, he is my mother's husband," I say. Just as matter-of-fact as that.

*What else can I say? Will this horror flick ever end? Is there something else they want from me? Would they like me to view other burnt bodies? Perhaps test me some more, see how much more I can endure before I crack?*

My thoughts interrupted by the doctor asking, "Do you want to remove your mother's ventilator?"

I respond, "Yes." I return to my mother's bedside and watch while her life support is removed.

One minute later, "Your mother's husband is officially dead." What seemed like only seconds after Artulo was pronounced dead, my mother breathed for the last time.

*Find something to hang on to. Hold on. Hold on.*

I find something.

They died within seconds or a minute of one another. They are together.

I don't feel any better.

I collapse in the waiting room, crying, my chest heaving. It doesn't matter that there are people staring at me from their vinyl hospital chairs. I bury my face in the couch. The cold vinyl feels good on my face, which is hot with perspiration. I hit the couch with my fist as hard as I can, over and over. I cry. Hit. Scream. Pound.

Finally, I'm exhausted. I'm not sure how I'm even walking. My husband is at my side, holding me upright, walking me out of the waiting room.

"Here are your mother's personal belongings," a hospital employee says.

I look at what's left. Her whole life in a plastic bag. All of her struggle to save money. All of her hard work. All of her sacrifices. Well, here it is. All in a plastic ziplock bag.

There's a wallet containing her driver's license. Her picture looks sad. A couple of twenty-dollar bills. A watch, burnt and bloody. A ripped leather jacket. That's all that's left.

Now I wish I had gone to eat with her at the Chinese restaurant. She asked me to go with her several times during the past few weeks. It's funny how one thinks of the silliest things at times like this—a simple request that I didn't think was important at the time. If only I had gone to eat Chinese food with her.

*My last memory. I want to remember. What did she look like? Was she happy? Were there signs that January 15, 2000, would be her last day on earth?* Never in my wildest dreams could I have prepared myself for this day.

*Let me think. Yes, she looked happy but sad. Yes, she knew that her life would end. The signs were there. In November 1999 she prepared a new will, making some changes. She wouldn't leave the Jehovah's Witness religious organization half of her property. Instead, she would leave her property to me, her only living daughter.*

\*\*\*

The last time I saw her was on January 14. I was getting ready for work. It was early morning, around six a.m. She called me. "Come over to my house; I need you sign something." I replied, "I'm in a hurry. I have to be at work early. "No, you come," she demanded.

I didn't feel like arguing with her, so on my way to work, I pulled in her driveway. She only lived across the street from me. I opened her front door, which she never locked, and called her name. She yelled that she was in her bedroom. I peeked into her bedroom but didn't see anyone. I heard her in her bathroom, adjacent to her bedroom. I called her name. She said to come to her bathroom.

She was putting on mascara. She looked pretty: nice hair, a wool suit, and freshly made up. It's funny what you remember at times like this. Her skirt was plaid and her jacket was brown. She said that she had to "take care of business today." She stopped putting on her mascara, turned around, and looked at me. She handed me two bank signature cards. She said, "I changee my bank account. I want you to be able to sign checks. Here, signee these cards."

I was a little irritated. I said, "You couldn't wait until I got off of work." "No," she said, matter-of-fact. "Just sign." I signed the cards. She reminded me that she wanted us to go to the Chinese restaurant that she had been talking about. "Very good."

"Okay, Mom, some other time we'll go," I said noncommittally.

When I left her house, she was standing at the front door. She looked sad. At the same time I thought, *She really is a beautiful woman.* That's my last image of her. Standing at the door, black hair softly brushing her face, distinct jaw line, large oval eyes, smiling.

Did she say she loved me? I'm not sure. But that wouldn't be like her. She didn't wear her emotions on her sleeve. It's not natural for Koreans to show their affection outwardly. But that day wasn't like any other. It was the eve of something ominous.

## CHAPTER 24

Soon I'm seeking answers. How did my mother die? Could I recreate her last moments? My uncle said that Mom's husband killed her. He knew they were fighting. He was still angry with my mother for marrying. He would miss stopping by his favorite sister's house to talk and eat.

My uncle and my mother enjoyed talking about business deals. They had a love/hate relationship, although my mother would never use such a strong term as hate. But they sure did get mad at one another. They would occasionally get into a shouting match, yelling profanities at top of their lungs, one talking over the other, neither one stopping for a breath.

Before Artulo entered the picture, my mother briefly dated a Korean man whose wife had died. He had five children. Because she refused to stop seeing him, Mom told me that her brother got so mad at her that he threw an ashtray at her, hitting her on the side of the head. While she could forgive her brother for that act, I couldn't, especially after years of her trying and finally succeeding to help her brother come to the U.S. to live a better life. Only a week after their fight, my mother and uncle were sitting at her kitchen table, eating rice and kimchee, and laughing, as if the ashtray incident didn't occur. I didn't understand their relationship.

Mom had also helped him start a couple of businesses. Of course, they never got anything straight regarding repayments of loans, and an argument would ensue. It got worse when they couldn't even agree upon the original loan amount.

These types of business dealings would drive me nuts, especially since I was asked to mediate and "get everything straighten out." It didn't pay to know how to read and write English in this Korean family.

\*\*\*

Now my uncle, who could be as stubborn and hotheaded as my mother, was insisting that I shouldn't bury my mother and Artulo together. He believed that Artulo murdered my mother.

Mom was planning to divorce Artulo. She had confided to me that she loved Artulo, but couldn't live with him. She said, "This time it is really going to hurt my heart."

The question lingers. Did Artulo accidentally or purposefully kill my mother?

I spoke to a tenant in the Washington, DC, building that had caught fire. The tenant ran a community center for substance abusers, a place where they could talk, drink coffee, and network. My mother would drop by the facility when she was in DC to collect overdue rent and even to contribute money. She'd always take time to socialize with the counselors and the folks using the facility.

The tenant said that my mother and Artulo had stopped by his office to have a cup of coffee and talk. They were on their way to another office space they had set up as an art studio. As usual, the tenant and my mother greeted one another warmly. The tenant offered them a cup of coffee, which they gladly accepted after being out in the cold January night.

The tenant said that Mom and Artulo were holding hands. "It was nice to see two people so much in love." After about a half hour of small talk, my mother and her husband said they were going to the art studio to work.

They walked up the stairs to their art studio. They were still holding hands and talking to one another, as if no one else existed.

Around ten p.m., the tenant heard a big bang, like an explosion. He shot up from his chair and ran up the stairs. The stairwell was filling up fast with smoke, making him cough and gag. As he reached the door to the art studio, he could see smoke pouring out of the crack under the door. He reached up to open the door, but it was locked. He stumbled down the stairs to the outside, gasping for air, and called 911.

The fire department arrived within minutes. By then, the roof of the building was ablaze, flames hungrily licking the thirty-year-old building. The brick turned black and the roof began crumbling. The firefighters rushed to the second floor of the building, where they rammed open the locked door.

In the studio, the ceiling was on fire. Two burnt bodies were lying on the floor. Artulo was still barely conscious. He'd managed to crawl to a window but collapsed before reaching it. My mother was lying by a work-table, unconscious. Sculpture molds and other sculpting equipment were lying on the table in disarray, blackened by the fire and smoke.

Artulo asked the firefighters about my mother, but I couldn't be sure of his exact words. I've heard two different accounts. The first was "Tell Moon I'm sorry." The other was "How is Moon?"

If the first account is accurate, what was he sorry about? Did he deliberately cause the explosion? Or perhaps he was just sorry that she was injured.

Or, as my uncle said, if my mother had never met Artulo, she'd be alive today.

What happened in that room?

Everyone was a suspect in my mind.

I wanted answers.

Was my uncle right? Was Mom murdered by her husband? I knew he was mentally ill. Did he stop taking his medication? Did he go off the deep end?

Mom had a temper. She could scream and yell loudly. She could make the calmest person explode. There was no stopping her when the floodgates opened. Could she have badgered Artulo to the point where he threw something at her to shut her up? Perhaps it was something that he was using to mold his sculpture with fire.

Another theory is that a drug addict followed them to the studio, robbed them, caused the explosion, locked the door from the outside, and left them for dead.

And there was the oldest motive in the world: greed and money. Could a business associate who was heavily in debt to her be the murderer? What about the tenant in the building? He owed her back rent totaling more than forty thousand dollars. Could that be motive enough?

The fire department came back with their findings. They concluded that my mother and her husband were using certain flammable devices for sculpturing. One such device exploded, and the explosion was so powerful and sudden that they didn't feel anything. The explosion occurred on a worktable in a small area, but it caused anything within its immediate vicinity and the ceiling above to instantly catch fire and burn.

The fire department concluded it was an accident. They never did confirm whether the studio door had been locked from the outside. But I heard that the door was so damaged when they forced their way into the studio that they couldn't conclude whether it was locked from the outside or not.

Artulo's adult children didn't agree with the firefighters' conclusion. They said that their father was too experienced with sculpting to have caused an explosion. They said, "Our father lived and breathed sculpting all of his life. Our family has been doing this for generations without any such accident."

While I believe the fire department's investigation to be accurate, I can also see the possibility of my mother and her husband becoming embroiled in an argument. They may have thrown things at each other, including the object that caused the explosion and fire. They were passionate in love and war.

But in the end, they were happy together. That is all that matters.

I don't blame anyone. I believe it was an accident, however it may have happened.

I believe my mother and her husband were deeply in love during the time they spent together.

CHAPTER 25

Today is the day we'll pay our last respects to my mother and her husband. Two small boxes holding their ashes are all that is left. I carefully place pictures around the boxes. I tear up as I look reminiscently at the framed photos. So many memories. My mother's pictures outnumber Artulo's pictures.

My favorite photo is when I graduated with my doctoral degree; my mother is beaming triumphantly, donning my blue graduation hat. Mom had said after the graduation ceremony, "I feel like I graduated. I so proud of you. Now I know my hard work pay off. I knew you could do whatever you wanted, but I didn't expect doctor degree possible for married woman. You work hard JUST like your mother. Maybe one day you write a book about your mother's life to help people know they can do more with their lives no matter how bad their lives are."

Another is a black-and-white photo of Mom, her little moon face smiling sweetly as a new immigrant first arriving in the U.S., eyes clear, hopeful, and innocent. Later, my mother, her square, strong-jawed face smiling confidently as she poses for the picture on a cruise ship, dressed in her floor-length, rose-colored gown. Her eyes have seen a lot. Last, my mother, the face of a woman who has experienced too much, sketched in charcoal by Artulo. Eyes of the living dead. Her husband's ghost has found a new home.

My mother's husband was born in Guatemala. He came from a family of artists and was, in fact, a well-respected artist in his country. He created intricate molds of horses in motion. They were wild and free, the artist's own desires reflected in his creations. Artulo didn't want to be tied down. Mom told me that he was happy roaming from one place to the other. He was uneasy about settling down. She said that he had a restless spirit—perhaps a demon that wouldn't allow him any peace.

This man had brought her so much happiness and hope for a peaceful life, just a year earlier, so much that she let her guard down—a feat she hadn't been able to accomplish for more than thirty years. She allowed herself to love again. To laugh again. To depend on someone other than herself for happiness. She married him for the right reasons and for the wrong reasons. Love was the right reason. Anger was the wrong reason.

When Mom gave of herself emotionally, it was a big deal. A huge deal. It meant she gave part of herself. She didn't understand the meaning of being detached. She was 100 percent involved.

***

This is the emotional attachment she had with her favorite niece, the daughter of her sister number four. The niece, her husband, and their daughter lived in her basement for approximately twelve years. It was roomy and comfortable. They had their own entrance, food preparation area, large closets, and a nice fireplace. Her niece and husband ran into some financial difficulty and couldn't keep their business, a gas station, afloat. My mother had lent them the money to buy the gas station, and she didn't want to lose her investment. So she bought the gas station from them.

Mom and Woon Gee decided to manage the gas station. Neither could read or write and both spoke broken English. Still, my mother would manage the day-to-day business while Woon Gee would repair cars.

But my mother was in way over her head. This was no carryout place. This wasn't rental property. Hard labor wouldn't do. The gas station was under a corporate giant, Chevron, which demanded proper bookkeeping and accounting. They demanded certain gas records be maintained. They wanted franchises to be managed according to their very detailed specifications. Policy and procedural manuals had to be adhered to. This was no mom-and-pop shop.

Along with the difficulty of keeping up the franchise paperwork, my mother's right leg, the one she injured when she fell on the greasy floor of the DC carryout location, began swelling. Pretty soon, she couldn't walk. Finally, my mother had to surrender and admit defeat.

As medical professionals had predicted in earlier incidences, the doctors said that there was a good possibility her leg would have to be amputated. They'd see how quickly it would heal from the aggressive antibiotic treatment she underwent. She remained in intensive care for a couple of weeks. Her leg remained elevated. IVs pumped a continuous stream of antibiotics into her body.

I just shook my head. My mother. When would she learn that her life was more important than losing a few bucks? She was no longer a starving, scared little girl in Korea. She owned property. She had enough income to live the American dream.

She eventually healed enough to return home, but she still had some fairly serious medical problems with her leg. She could no longer work eighteen hours a day. She hired her niece and her niece's husband to work at the gas station. She didn't have a choice. Woon Gee quit; I'm not certain why. With all of the gas station debts paid, her niece asked my mother to reinstate her as the owner. My mother conceded, but not without a hitch. She wanted the old and new debt paid off with interest. Her niece agreed.

Her niece paid her monthly payments when she could, but she also had another obligation: herself. She liked to shop. After all, she was the owner of a gas station. She had to dress like a business owner. As her payments became more erratic, Mom would remind her of the amount she owed. She got deeper and deeper in debt to my mother, and their recollection of how much was paid and owed became further and further apart. The niece claimed that my mother charged too high an interest rate. Mom argued that she could have lent the money to many other Korean business associates at higher interest rates. They could not reconcile the outstanding balance.

They began arguing, and the arguments turned personal. My mother pointed out her niece's spending habits. She would say, "Why you spend money on another dress? You try to act like big shot." Her niece would respond, "I don't want to look like a *coogee* (beggar) woman like you!" My mother would cry. "Why you want to hurt my feelings like that?" And they would go back and forth for the next year or more. The closeness they once felt for one another turned to hatred.

Finally, my mother hired an attorney, which was unheard of among Korean families. She was going after "them" tooth and nail. Her niece hurt her. My mother used to tell me that this "fight" hurt her more than anything she'd experienced, because she loved her niece so much. I wasn't privy to all of the details, but I hadn't seen my mother so emotionally distraught since my father wrote his "farewell and kiss my behind" letter so long ago.

It wasn't about the money. Other failed business associates owed her a hundred times more than what her niece had borrowed. But this was personal. She knew that succeeding in a business was somewhat of a gamble. Some made it; others didn't. But she didn't understand how her favorite niece could talk to her in such a disrespectful manner.

Mom's niece moved out of her home after twelve years of living together. Their relationship was so strained that they could no longer talk to one another without shouting.

My mother would ask me to take her side. I reminded Mom that she had loaned money to relatives in the past, where repayment disagreements arose. I had asked her not to lend money to relatives, and that if she did and they didn't repay her, then she needed to forget it. She hadn't listened to me—again. I told her, "I don't want to be involved in this chaos. I can't stand to see you angry, bitter, upset, and sick over a stupid mistake you keep making. You never learn."

My mother yelled, "Well, you educated! I not. How come you can't help me? You write them letter. Tell them they owe me money and they hurt me."

I responded, "No. I'm tired of getting in the middle of your self-imposed chaos and hurt. You did it to yourself. I can't even make heads or tails out of your bookkeeping."

"I try to help my niece. Why she try to hurt me so much? Now my daughter hurt me."

Guilt. Nope, she wasn't putting that one on me. But I felt sorry for her. Who doesn't want to help their mother?

"You cold fish! My daughter cold fish!" my mother would shout.

Guilt again. Nope, I still wouldn't be responsible for how she was feeling.

Finally, Mom turned and left my house. She didn't talk to me for days. Then she'd come around again when she needed me to read something for her. Or prepare another lease. Or write an eviction notice.

I could see that my mother was hurting. When she hurt, I hurt. That's why I had to stop this emotional roller coaster. I wanted to help her, just as I had as a child when my father left. But how long must I suffer because she suffered? And she seemed to be very comfortable suffering and being hurt.

If I couldn't change her, then I had to change me. That meant I had to separate us emotionally. Like Siamese twins who share organs and tissues that might result in the death of one, I had to cut off the emotional reservoir that we shared. My mother was on her own. I was on my own. We would be two separate adults who would live and die by our own choices in life.

My mother became increasingly depressed about her relationship with her niece. Now she felt as though I had abandoned her. She wanted to be loved and protected. That's when she decided. Just like her real estate buying decisions. Last minute. Must do. Not next year. Not next month. Not next week. Not tomorrow. Now. Must do now. She must be married. That was the answer. No one would push around a woman with a husband. Her husband would take her side. United, they would be strong.

\*\*\*

Her family pleaded with her not to marry a younger man. They told her that she was too old to remarry, that she should be content, that he was marrying her for her money. My mother's brother cursed her, calling her bad names.

Mom just became more determined to marry. Her family's reaction was exactly why she wanted to marry. Certainly, they wouldn't talk to her that way if she were married.

When she brought her new husband to my home, they were holding hands. I've never seen my mother giggle and smile at a man. I thought it was about time she was happy. Her new husband didn't look younger. They just seemed perfect together. He couldn't keep his hands off her: brushing her hair, touching her hand, patting her on the leg. Yes, they looked just like two love-struck teenagers.

A few months passed, and Mom said she needed to tell me something. "Keep this a secret. I know I don't listen to anyone. But I have to tell you something about my husband." I could tell by her tone of voice that something was wrong. Dreadfully wrong.

My mother looked scared. She talked in lower tones. "My husband possess by ghost. He wake up at night and talk to himself. I watch him from my bed. He walks back and forth. Like a ghost. The next morning when he in shower, I look in his suitcase. I see a prescription bottle. Some kind of medicine. I don't know what it is. I write the name. See, here it is. I write it right here."

I looked at the name. I thought I recognized it, though I wasn't certain from where. I thought hard.

Then I remembered. Oh my God. I couldn't believe it. This was the same medicine that my husband's uncle took for schizophrenia.

I told my mother.

She didn't speak. She'd met the schizophrenic uncle over the years. She'd always felt sorry for him.

She was visibly shaken. "Don't tell anyone. I hardheaded. I don't listen to anyone. My family tell me not to marry. I marry anyway."

I asked, "What are you going to do?"

My mother said, "I love him. I never let any man love me. But this man, I let in my heart. If we not together, I very, very hurt. More hurt than when your father leave me."

I asked, "Are you going to say anything to him?"

She said, "I talk to him later."

My practical mind kicked in. "Did he sign the prenuptial?"

My mother hung her head. "No."

I couldn't believe it. She'd done it again, jumped into something as important as marriage without the paperwork in order. *Stupid, stupid, stupid.* But I didn't say the words aloud. I didn't want to rub salt in my mother's wounds. I hoped and prayed they were just wounds. She could be fatally injured if things didn't turn around.

Another week passed. My mother updated me on her marriage. Her husband didn't want material things. He wanted to be free to roam as he pleased, just like the wild horses he created. He'd told her that he would be perfectly happy sitting under a tree or roaming the earth, reveling in its beauty.

My mother couldn't comprehend a life without roots and purpose. A talented artist sitting under a tree? No, that just would be a waste of a God-given talent. She was going to set him up in business. She wasn't a bad artist herself—no surprise, since her right brain seemed to be the only side operating.

Artulo continued to transform into a ghost every night. Eventually, the ghost appeared in the daytime: the ghost of depression. His youthful face would age twenty years. His half-cocked smile turned downward. A grayish tint dulled his skin. The world was crashing all around him. The next day, he would change back to the man she married—kind, loving, caring.

My mother accepted the dual personality, convinced that she would change him and get rid of the ghost. My mother decided to set up a business for him on the second floor of her building in Washington, DC, the building that would later be their "oven."

A nonprofit drug-counseling center rented the upstairs and downstairs. The organization was behind in its rent. She put up with the rent deficit because she thought they were doing a good deed. She talked to the founder of the drug rehabilitation center and convinced him to move his operations downstairs and pay less rent. She'd use the upstairs. That would be the start of their new art studio. Her husband could set up shop and sculpture his horse statues. They were in business.

At some point—I can't even tell when, but not too much later—my mother paid me a visit with another update. "My husband and I separate. We cannot get along. He has too many ghosts. He not happy. Now he ask me to pay him twenty-five thousand dollars to leave."

I said, "What happened to the free spirit who doesn't care about material things?" My mother acted as though she didn't hear me, lost in her own rambling. "I not pay him. I mad. How can he ask for my money? I work hard for my money. He not going to get it. He say he doesn't want money. Now he say he wants money. I buy him car. I pay to fix his home in Guatemala. I don't mind give him money. But he ask. Now I don't want to give him money. He hurt me."

Instead of feeling sorry for her, I just grew angry. *Stupid, stupid, stupid,* I kept saying over and over in my head.

As if she heard me, she said, "I am stupid. I hardhead. Why I never listen to anyone?"

She looked dejected. Then, she stood up from my kitchen table and simply left. No fanfare. No tears. No yelling.

I sat there, like a cold fish. Cold fish don't feel. I didn't want to feel. I was a cold fish. No feeling, no hurt.

## CHAPTER 26

People just pour in the funeral parlor door. I think, *Where are they all coming from?* Koreans, African Americans, Caucasians, Hispanic, every race is represented. The funeral director has to open the partition to another room, then another, to accommodate the crowd.

The funeral director asks if anyone would like to make a statement. The first to rise is my mother's tenant in the DC building, the one who saw her last. He is a tall African American man with close-cropped hair and wearing a Muslim prayer cap. He is humble in appearance and manner.

"Moon was a good woman. She cared about my organization. She would attend our AA meetings and donate money." Sob. "She was like my mama. She was always trying to help me out. Talk to me like I was her son." Sob. "I'm gonna miss her. I was the last one to have a cup of coffee with her." Sob.

Others stand, one after another. They each have a story to tell. She has made an impact on many lives. She opened herself up to them. She allowed them to be part of her life. She gave freely of herself. She was brutally frank with people who couldn't pull themselves off the streets, but they loved her because her frankness came from a place of caring. Of loving. She made a difference in their lives, regardless of race and socioeconomic background. She was honest through and through.

I have always known that about my mother. She was raw. This is why she hurt most of her life. If she was mad, you'd know it. If she was happy, you'd know it. If she was sad, you'd know it. She lived life without hypocrisy. She saw people for themselves, not the cost of the fabric on their back or the size of their diamond or how much money they had in their bank accounts or what model of car they drove. It was black or white. You were bad or good. You were bad if you lied and stole. You were good if you told the truth and worked for your needs and desires. Simple as that.

Regardless of peoples' baggage, if they were good, she could see it. She believed in the goodness of people because she came from a place of honesty and godliness.

My mother believed in the goodness of her husband, Artulo, ghosts and all. She understood how he felt—she had her share of pain—the kind that cut so deeply in her soul, they never healed completely. "I want to be with my husband until the day I die. I love him, even if it hurts my heart. Dying would be better than to live without his love. What's life without love?"

Their headstone is absent of birth dates. It makes no difference. Their lives began the day they shed their tired bodies. The sensitive minds and bodies of two good people who weren't able to rid themselves of suffering while in earthly form. Now, they can live and love unfettered by the ghosts of their past.

Sadness. Go in peace.
Abuse. Go in peace.
Betrayal. Go in peace.
Illness. Go in peace.
Murder. Go in peace.
Death. Go in peace.
Ghosts. Go in peace.
Newlyweds. Go in peace and love freely!

Their burial headstone is marked simply:

ARTULO TALA MORATAYA
AND
MOON-JA CATELLIER
FOREVER IN LOVE
January 15, 2000